Edited by
Anna Jackson

V&A A Hundred Highlights

V&A

Introduction

Museums collect, conserve and display objects, to inform, educate and delight their visitors. The great museums of the world are boundless sources of pleasure and instruction and nowhere is this more true than in the Victoria and Albert Museum. Our collections are so rich and so diverse that an unsuspecting visitor may be in danger of drowning in an uncharted sea of objects, cultures and periods. This Guide is intended to help you navigate the galleries, and provides some key points of reference for each of the collections.

The Museum was born of the cultural idealism of the mid-nineteenth century. Britain at this time was a land of considerable prosperity for some, but grinding poverty for many more. Political stability and world power status caused the leaders of society to argue that life for everyone could be continuously improved through education and example. The origins of the V&A lie in this belief. After years of debate the Museum was finally founded in 1852, following the enormous success of the Great Exhibition the previous year. Profits from the Exhibition were used to establish the new institution, exhibits were purchased to form the basis of its collections and Henry Cole, one of the masterminds of the 1851 event, was chosen to be the first Director. The Museum of Manufactures, as it was initially called, aimed to make works of art available to all, to educate the working population and to inspire British designers and manufacturers. The first home of the Museum was Marlborough House, near Buckingham Palace, but in 1857 it moved to its present site and was renamed The South Kensington Museum. Under the guidance of the Superintendent of Collections, John Charles Robinson, the Museum expanded rapidly. Using his considerable expertise, Robinson set out to acquire the best examples of decorative art from all periods. He also added what is traditionally regarded as fine art, that is painting, drawing, prints and sculpture, with which to further illuminate the history of art and design.

The Museum itself also grew, although in a somewhat haphazard fashion, with new buildings being erected as and when needed. Many of these buildings, with their iron frames and glass roofs, were intended to be semi-permanent exhibition halls, but they have all survived and comprise one of the finest groups of Victorian buildings in Britain. In 1899 Queen Victoria laid the foundation stone of a new building designed to give the Museum a grand facade and main entrance. To mark the occasion it was renamed The Victoria and Albert Museum, in memory of the enthusiastic support Prince Albert had given to its foundation. The new building, by Aston Webb, was opened in 1909 and is today the familiar exterior of the Museum.

Throughout the twentieth century the collections have continued to grow, making the V&A the greatest museum of decorative arts in the world. The incredible collections of ceramics, glass, textiles, dress, silver, ironwork, jewellery, furniture, sculpture, paintings, prints and photographs span the cultures of Europe, North America, Asia and North Africa, and date from ancient times to the present day.

Much of what goes on here is still true to the spirit of our Victorian founders. As you go around the Museum you may well come across groups of students studying particular aspects of design or sketching in the galleries. Behind the scenes are hundreds of experts, including curators, conservators, researchers and teachers, all using the collections to advance our knowledge. We work closely with schools, universities, adult education colleges and community groups throughout the country and abroad to develop the understanding and appreciation of the decorative arts of the world. I think Prince Albert and Henry Cole would approve of the way their museum continues to fulfil the purposes for which it was established.

For our visitors the V&A is a glorious treasure house, filled with amazing and beautiful objects. This Guide will help you discover some of these delights and will provide a souvenir of a unique institution. It is my pleasure to welcome you here, but perhaps I should also issue a gentle warning: the V&A is an enchanting and bewitching place. It casts a spell which few can escape, and having set foot in here you want to come back and see just a little more. Few spells can be more alluring or more rewarding.

Alan Borg

ALAN BORG
Director

How to Use this Guide

The V&A is one of the largest museums in the world with tens of thousands of objects on display in its seven miles of galleries. This Guide gives a taste of the amazing variety of objects exhibited in the Museum by introducing 100 of the most significant and spectacular things to see.

The V&A's collections are displayed in different types of galleries. Some, such as the 20th Century Gallery and the European Galleries, are designed to show the visual relationship between objects from the same country or historical period. Others, like the Glass Gallery and the Silver Gallery, are devoted to objects of one specific type and show developments in form, function and technique. Some galleries are dedicated to one group of particularly important objects, such as the Raphael Cartoons and the Devonshire Hunting Tapestries.

This book aims to guide you around these galleries via some of the wonderful objects on display. The Museum is a very large place, so it is not a good idea to try to look at everything in one visit. We recommend that you choose what you would most like to see from the list **overleaf**, or by flicking through the pages that follow to see what catches your eye.

The Museum is constantly improving its displays and facilities so there may well be occasions when galleries are closed. Objects that are sensitive to light cannot be exhibited for long periods of time and so are regularly changed. Objects are also removed for conservation or for loan to exhibitions in other museums. These activities may mean that specific objects illustrated in this Guide are not on display at the time of your visit, but we hope that the many exciting alternatives will relieve any disappointment.

NOTE

Following a successful lottery bid, the British Galleries have been closed for extensive refurbishment and redesign. The new galleries will reopen in late 2001. From time to time adjacent galleries will also have to be closed for enabling works. Key objects from the British Galleries can be seen in a *Best of British* display in Gallery 62.

These maps will help you find your way around. The main body of the Museum consists of four levels. There are six levels in the Henry Cole Wing. Hanging in the galleries are large colour-coded banners: red banners direct you north, yellow to the east, green to the south and blue to the west.

Free detailed maps, including all facilities, are available from the Information Desks, and if you need help at any time please ask any member of Museum staff.

Henry Cole Wing

Level
6
5
4
3
2
1

Level **A**

Morris Room   Gamble Room   Poynter Room

North Court

Restaurant

Shop

| 11 | 12 | 13 | 14 | 15 | 16 |

Italy
1400–1500

27

17

28

18
Italy

26   29

Exhibition Courts

38   38A   39

19

Ramp to Lower Level

Galleries 1–7

20

Garden

Northern Europe

25
Spain

32   33

51
Sculpture

Exhibition Road Entrance

| 21 | **Europe 1500–1600** | 21A | 22 | 23 | **Europe 1100–1450** | 24 |

46A
Cast Courts

46B
Cast Courts

1A-C
Europe 1600–1800

40
Dress

41
India

42
Islamic

43
Medieval Treasury

44
China

45
Japan

46   **Fakes & Forgeries**

2A-B

47A   **South East Asia/ India**   47B   47C   47D   47E   **China**   47F   47G   **Korea**

3A-D

48A
Raphael

Shop

50A   **Sculpture & Architecture**   50B

4   5A-C   **Europe**   6   7A-E   **Europe 1600–1800**

Europe & America 1800–1900

8   9

Friends Office & Room Picture Library

Secretariat Gate

Cromwell Road Entrance

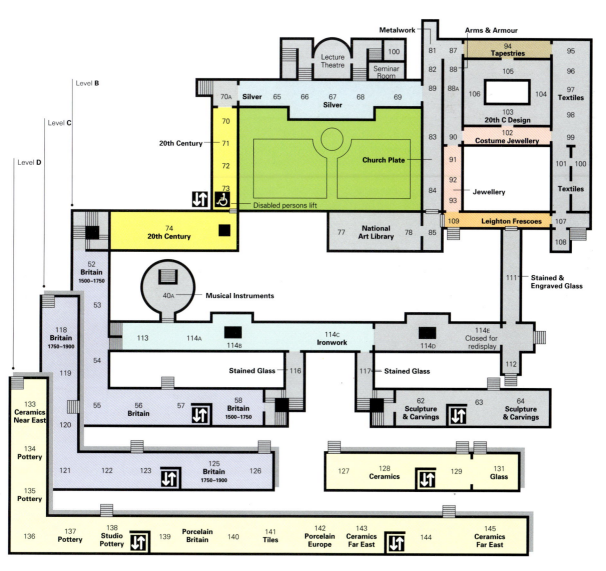

The European Galleries

The European Galleries contain the V&A's superlative collection of European art, dating from the Middle Ages through to the end of the nineteenth century. The earliest objects were made in about AD 400, when Christianity was becoming established as the dominant religion. The majority of the objects that survive from the early medieval period were housed in the treasuries of the great churches and cathedrals. Many were created to inspire and aid Christian devotion, and are decorated with images from biblical texts and the lives of the saints. The ivory panels of the **Veroli casket (1)**, however, are decorated with scenes of classical mythology. This casket was formerly in the Cathedral Treasury at Veroli, south-east of Rome, but was made in Constantinople (now Istanbul) in the late tenth or early eleventh century. The Roman Empire was divided between west and east in AD 293. While Roman authority crumbled in western Europe the Byzantine Empire continued to

The Gloucester Candlestick (2) is one of the great masterpieces of medieval art. First modelled in wax, it was then cast in three sections, and is made of copper, zinc, tin, lead, nickel, iron, antimony, arsenic and silver. The unusual proportions of this mixture may suggest that the candlestick was made from a hoard of old coins. Of three Latin inscriptions on the candlestick, the most important is the one which refers to its donation: 'The devotion of abbot Peter and his gentle flock gave me to the church of St Peter at Gloucester'. Peter was Abbot of the Benedictine monastery of St Peter, now Gloucester Cathedral, from 1104 until his death in 1113. The fantastic composition of men, monsters and foliage seen on the candlestick was common to much northern European art of this date, but the style indicates that this piece was made in England, possibly in Canterbury.

As with much medieval art, these **plaques (3)** are enigmatic in purpose and even in subject. The man grappling the lion is probably the Old Testament hero Samson, although it

1. The Veroli Casket
The Medieval Treasury,
Room 43
216-1865

expand and prosper, and it was here that the heritage of classical antiquity was cherished and preserved throughout the Middle Ages. The strength and stability of the Empire encouraged the growth of all branches of the arts, and by the end of the tenth century ivory carving was flourishing. This beautifully carved casket was probably made for a person close to the Imperial Court in Constantinople, the capital of the Empire, and may have been used to hold scent bottles or jewellery.

could be the classical hero Hercules who also had an epic fight with a lion. Another plaque shows Alexander the Great, whose exploits were reinvented by medieval artists and writers. Here he is shown riding across the skies in a chariot pulled by mythical beasts known as griffins. These plaques, which date to about 1150, are close in style and size to a number of others now scattered across Europe. It is likely that they all originally came from one great work of art, possibly an altarpiece, which was

**2. The Gloucester
Candlestick**
The Medieval Treasury,
Room 43
◀ 7649-1861

3. Enamel plaques
The Medieval Treasury,
Room 43
M.53-1988 ▶

broken up as a result of war or revolution. The
plaques are enamelled in *champlevé*, one of the
most important decorative techniques of the
Middle Ages. The copper base of each plaque
was deeply engraved with a design, and the
cavities filled with coloured powder made from
ground glass. The plaque was then fired at a
very high temperature, polished and gilded.
The range, depth and subtlety of colours make
these plaques some of the greatest examples of
medieval enamelling. They were probably
made in one of the well-established metalwork-
ing centres such as Liège or Maastricht.

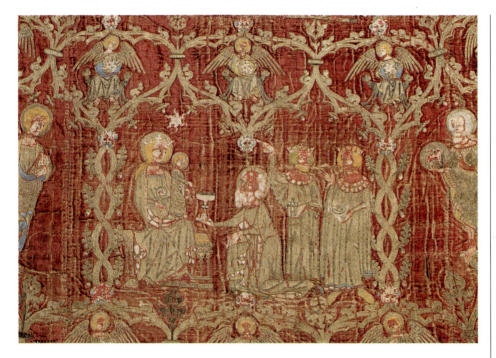

The **Butler-Bowden Cope (4)** derives its name from the family who owned it for several centuries, and is a superb example of medieval ecclesiastical embroidery from the Museum's unrivalled collection of *Opus Anglicanum* or 'English work'. This sumptuous ceremonial church vestment dates from around 1330-50 and shows scenes from the Life of the Virgin with apostles and saints, embroidered with silver, silver-gilt thread and silk, on a rich crimson velvet. One of the most luxurious types of work produced in England in the thirteenth and fourteenth centuries, *Opus Anglicanum* was much coveted by the most powerful people in Europe including kings and popes, and was used as a forceful visual statement of their wealth and status. Many medieval church vestments were later cut up and re-used. This cope, as can be seen from its dismembered state, was made into a variety of ecclesiastical garments, but was re-assembled in the nineteenth century.

The rapid changes that took place in European culture in the period around 1500 are reflected in the nature and style of both secular and religious art. The extraordinary **Burghley Nef (5)** was made in Paris in 1527-8. In medieval France the word *Nef* was applied to various types of boat-shaped vessel, including the most magnificent objects intended for the dining tables and buffets of the rich. Apart from having an obvious ornamental quality, their function was to hold personal pieces of cutlery or, as in this case, salt. A highly valued commodity at the time, salt was worthy of the most costly materials. This nautilus shell, mounted in silver, was a rare natural curiosity. The Burghley Nef would have been placed in front of the most important person at table as a mark of their status. At the foot of the mast are the tiny figures of the lovers Tristan and Iseult playing chess who, according to the legend, mistakenly drank a love potion and suffered tragic consequences.

Changes in devotional practices in the latter Middle Ages led to the emergence of various distinctive forms of religious image. The route to salvation became increasingly stressed in terms of personal devotion and individual communion with God, and **Books of Hours (6)** such as this early sixteenth-century example from northern France, were widely owned. These books were used during the recitation of prayers at prescribed times of day – known as the liturgical 'hours' – the pictures helping to focus the mind on events in the Virgin's life. This particular page shows the Adoration of the Magi, which was a standard image for the liturgical midday hour known as Sext. The traditional composition, widely used in the fifteenth century, has here been given a 'modern' Renaissance architectural frame. The production of these texts was the basis of a flourishing book trade even before 1486, when large numbers of densely illustrated Books of Hours began to be printed in Paris. Handmade versions, such as this one, were still produced by scribes and illuminators, however, although by the 1530s they were working mainly for a luxury market.

Another, more public, form of religious image that became common in Europe at this time was the altarpiece with hinged wings. *Mary Salome and Zebedee* (**7**) by Tilman Riemenschneider (*c*.1460-1531) originally formed the right wing of an altarpiece showing the family of the Virgin Mary. The central scene would have shown St Anne seated with her daughter Mary and the Christ Child. Mary Salome was another daughter of St Anne, half-sister of the Virgin and wife of Zebedee. Tilman Riemenschneider was one of the most important sculptors in southern Germany in the late fifteenth and early sixteenth century. He specialized in carving limewood altarpieces, some of which were painted. Others, such as this example which was carved in Würzburg in about 1501-5, were given a translucent glaze. This treatment not only allowed the rich colour of the wood to show through, but rendered the fine carving of the faces and drapery rather more visible.

By the later Middle Ages the churches and cathedrals of northern Europe had grown considerably in size and opulence. This stained glass window, dating from the end of the fifteenth century, depicts **Joanna of Aragon (8)**. Joanna was the heiress to the Spanish throne, the wife of Philip the Handsome, Count of Flanders, and the daughter-in-law of Maximilian of Austria, Holy Roman Emperor and ruler of the Netherlands. She is remembered, however, not for her illustrious status, but for her irrational behaviour which earned her the title 'Joanna the Mad.' This window is one of a series depicting Joanna, Philip, Maximilian and other members of their family, which they gave to the Chapel of the Holy Blood in the church of St Basil at Bruges. The Chapel was maintained by the Brotherhood of the Holy Blood, an organization of local citizens carrying out good works, who used it for their services. Although much restored, the rich colours and detailing on the remaining original glass make it one of the finest examples to survive from the period.

7. *Mary Salome and Zebedee* by **Riemenschneider**
Northern Europe, Room 27
110-1878

8. Joanna of Aragon
Northern Europe,
Room 28
C.442-1918 ▶

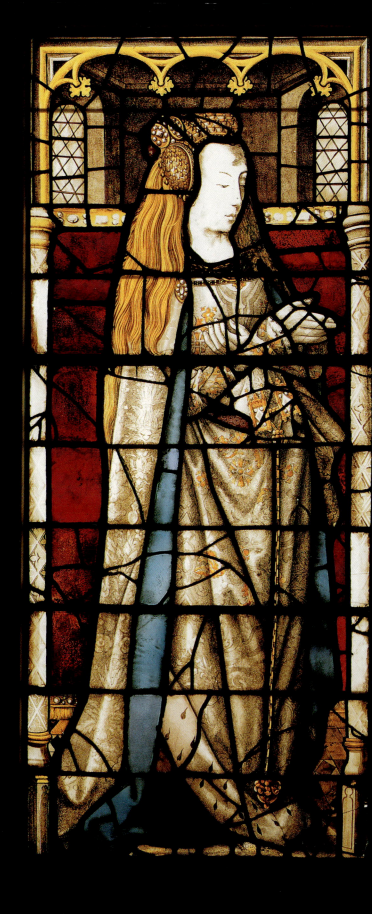

The signature on the back of this particular *maiolica* plate (10) indicates that it was painted by 'jacopo'. Dating to about 1510, it is the most fully signed piece of the Cafaggiolo workshop and is superbly decorated with a scene from the Old Testament story of Judith and Holofernes. Judith was a Jewish heroine who, during the seige of the city of Bethulia by the Assyrians, entered the enemy camp and managed to seduce and behead their general Holofernes. She was adopted by the Florentine Republic as a heroine and a slayer of tyrants, and is shown here as a contemporary Florentine lady carrying a banner with the colours of the city.

The Renaissance, or rebirth, of classical culture that flourished in Italy in the fifteenth and sixteenth centuries was a period of exceptional artistic achievement. This bronze roundel, with its intimate portrayal of **The Virgin and Child with Four Angels** (9), is by the Florentine artist Donatello (*c.*1386-1466), the most celebrated and influential Italian sculptor of the fifteenth century. The roundel was given by the artist to his doctor, Giovanni Chellini, who wrote about it in his daybook of 27 August 1456. The reverse is hollowed out, creating a mould for casting replicas of the image in molten glass. In order to test this unique feature, copies of the roundel were made from which glass versions were cast, one of which is on display in the back of the case.

One of Donatello's most important patrons was Cosimo de Medici. The Medici were the most powerful family of the Florentine Republic and under their patronage the arts flourished. Some of the finest Renaissance ceramics were produced in Cafaggiolo, north of Florence, in a pottery attached to a villa owned by the Medici. The type of tin-glazed earthenwares made there are known as *maiolica*.

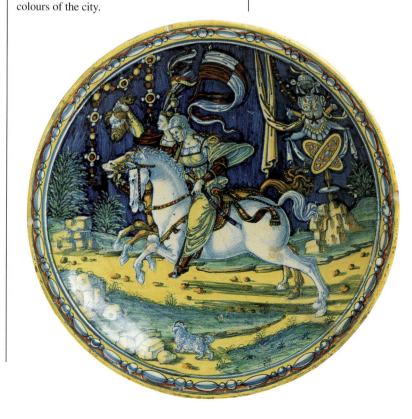

The Adoration of the Magi (11) is by the Florentine sculptor Andrea della Robbia (1435-1525). Andrea inherited the family workshop from his famous uncle, Luca della Robbia, who had developed the technique of applying tin glazes, similar to those used by potters, to terracotta (fired clay) to produce sculptures that were colourful, durable and relatively cheap. Larger sculptures, such as this example which dates to about 1500-10, were made in sections in order to fit into the kiln for firing. The scene is set in a landscape, showing the Three Kings with attendants, offering their gifts to the Holy Family. Andrea's sculpture was similar in style to contemporary painting, but certain colours, such as red, could not be produced in tin-glaze. The coat-of-arms of the Albizzi, a prominent Florentine family, can be seen on the frame, and the relief was probably commissioned by them for a church not far from Florence. The shiny surface of the altarpiece would have reflected the candle-light in the chapel, bringing the image to life.

Andrea Briosco (c.1470-1532), the artist of *The Shouting Horseman* (12), had a mass of curly hair and was generally known by his nickname Riccio, meaning Curly Head. Riccio was acknowledged as a master of the bronze statuette and in this sculpture, made in Padua in about 1510-15, he created a remarkable sense of movement and tension. The pose of the group may have been inspired by the Venetian light cavalry, who rode bareback, or by a description of a lively and agitated horse published by one of Riccio's friends in 1504. Bronzes are usually made so that they can be reproduced in several versions, but the method of casting used by Riccio makes this horse and rider unique. The group came to light at the end of the nineteenth century when it was owned by Frédéric Spitzer, a French collector who was notorious for faking silver objects and armour. Spitzer almost certainly arranged for copies of the rider to be made as these exist in some numbers displayed on a variety of horses.

12. *The Shouting Horseman* by Riccio
Italy, Room 12
▼ A.88-1910

13. The Morris and Gamble Refreshment Rooms ▶

Running alongside the Italian Renaissance Galleries are the Museum's three original **refreshment rooms (13)** which date from the 1860s. The Green Dining Room was designed by William Morris (1834–96). Although now recognized as one of the most important designers and thinkers of his day, Morris was still relatively unknown when his firm was commissioned to decorate the room. The stained glass windows and the painted panels are by the artist Edward Burne-Jones (1833–98), a friend and associate of Morris. James Gamble (1835–1919), one of the Museum's own design team, was responsible for the central room. The dazzling ceramic tiles which adorn the walls and columns were chosen for practical as well as decorative reasons, as they would resist fire, steam, the smell of food and be easy to clean. The frieze that runs around the room quotes from the Book of Ecclesiasticus 2:24, while appetizing sayings decorate the stained glass windows.

The last room is dominated by the iron and brass grill which was used to cook chops and steaks. This, and the surrounding blue-and-white tiles, were designed by the artist Edward Poynter (1836–1919). These three rooms catered for Museum visitors every day until the outbreak of World War II. Subsequently used as stores, the rooms were restored to their former glory in the 1970s.

Samson Slaying a Philistine (14) is the earliest of the great marble groups by Giambologna (1529-1608), sculptor to the Medici Grand Dukes of Tuscany, and the only substantial work by the artist to have left Italy. It was commissioned, in about 1562, by Francesco de Medici for a fountain in Florence, but was later sent as a gift to Spain. The group was presented to the Prince of Wales, later King Charles I, in 1623 while he was in Spain negotiating a marriage contract, and it soon became the most famous Italian sculpture in England. The dramatic pose is based on a composition by Michelangelo, who was in his late seventies when Giambologna met him in Rome. A masterpiece of artistic and technical virtuosity, the group was carved from just one block of marble, supported on only five narrow points. Over the years these fractured under the weight of the figures, so the sculpture has been strengthened by inserting metal rods into the legs of the Philistine.

While such grandiose marble statues were conceived as monuments of public splendour, objects such as this **spinet (15)** were used to enhance private status. Possibly the most lavishly decorated keyboard instrument to survive, the spinet was made in 1577 by the Milanese craftsman Annibale Rossi (active 1542-77). Embellished with nearly 2000 precious stones, it is an early example of *pietre dure*, or 'hard stone', decoration. The style of the ivory motifs surrounding the stones is derived from a form of ornament known as *strap work*, which was used at the Palace of Fontainebleau in France in the 1530s. Influential styles such as this were rapidly circulated around European artistic centres in the form of engravings. This spinet was shown at the Paris Exposition of 1867, and subsequently acquired by the Museum for the then enormous sum of £1,200.

14. *Samson Slaying a Philistine* by **Giambologna**
Europe 1500-1600, Room 21
A.7-1954

15. Spinet by Rossi
Europe 1600-1800,
Room 1a
809-1869

**16. *Thomas Baker*
by Bernini**
Europe 1600-1800,
Room 1c
A.63-1921

The bust of ***Thomas Baker* (16)** was made by the great Baroque sculptor, Gian Lorenzo Bernini (1598-1680), who revolutionized portrait sculpture with his vivid characterization. Thomas Baker (1606-58) is shown with flowing hair and an elaborate lace collar. Baker travelled extensively in Europe, commissioning this bust after visiting Bernini's studio in Rome in 1636. Baker was well-connected with English court circles, and may have taken Anthony van Dyck's famous triple-portrait of King Charles I to Rome, for Bernini to use as a model for his marble bust of the king. When the Pope, who was Bernini's patron, heard that the sculptor was working on Thomas Baker's portrait without his permission, he forbade him to continue. It was later finished with the help of a workshop assistant, who was largely responsible for the lower portion. At one time the bust belonged to Sir Peter Lely, the principal court painter to King Charles II and himself a specialist in portraiture.

This magnificent silver **ewer and basin (17)**, of 1621-2, is decorated with episodes from the life of Giovanni Grimaldi, who was a member of one of the most important aristocratic families in seventeenth-century Genoa. The ewer depicts the battle of the River Po in 1431, at which Giovanni commanded the Milanese fleet against the Venetians. Also prominent on the set are the arms of the Lomellini, another highly influential Genoese family whose wealth was partly founded on trade in coral. There is no documentary evidence for the commission but the two dynasties shared trading interests and were related by marriage. It may be that the pieces were made for the Grimaldi but later passed on to the Lomellini, perhaps as a wedding gift or to mark a business transaction. Objects such as these were deliberately designed to be admired rather than used. The sculptural decoration of the set, in particular the writhing handle and shell lip of the ewer, reflects the taste for marine and grotesque ornament that was fashionable in the sixteenth and early seventeenth centuries.

This **panel (18)** is one of a set of four that were made in about 1710 specifically for display as wall hangings. The workmanship is French, but they are Russian in origin and may have been made by French embroiderers in St Petersburg to cater for the deeply Francophile taste of the Russian court in this period. The canvas panels are embroidered with wools and silks in an intriguing variety of motifs. They have a loose framework of exotic foliage similar to the highly fashionable patterns, known as *bizarre*, of contemporary French woven silks. Scattered within these swathes of colour and movement are tiny scenes. These include still lifes with fruit and blue-and-white porcelain, garden statues and urns in the style of those used to ornament the gardens of the Palace of Versailles, and genre figures based on the paintings and tapestry designs of the Flemish artist David Teniers the Younger (1610-90).

One of the most sought after luxury items in seventeenth-century Europe was porcelain imported from China and Japan. The first European factory to make such porcelain successfully was established in Meissen in 1710. Although the secret of porcelain production soon spread to other European centres, the supremacy of Meissen's ceramics remained unchallenged for many decades. In the 1720s the Meissen factory began to produce richly decorated table services which soon came to replace silver as grand diplomatic gifts. The **Möllendorff dinner service (19)** originally consisted of over 960 pieces. Divided up in the nineteenth century, groups of it are now held in both public and private collections world-wide. The service was designed in about 1762 by Frederick II the Great, King of Prussia (1712-86), in collaboration with Karl Jacob Christian Klipfel, a Meissen artist and musician. Some of the figures were modelled by Johann Joachim Kändler (1706-75). The factory's renown was in great part due to the ingenuity of Kändler, a court sculptor who became chief modeller for Meissen and worked there for 42 years. The service was presented to the Prussian Major-General (later Field Marshal) Richard Joachim Heinrich von Möllendorff (1724-1816), as a reward for his military achievements during Frederick II's Seven Years War (1756-63) against Austria for possession of Silesia.

The factory at Meissen was founded by the passionate collector Augustus II. This elaborate **writing cabinet (20)** was made in about 1750-5 for his son Frederick Augustus III (1696-1763), Elector of Saxony and King of Poland. A celebrated example of German Rococo cabinet-making, it exemplifies the genre in its sophisticated choice of materials and workmanship. Augustus III's court looked to Paris for artistic inspiration, but the complex marquetry of wood, mother-of-pearl, ivory and brass, together with the elaborate gilt mounts of this piece, are equal in quality to any French counterpart. The cabinet was made at one of the leading Dresden workshops, possibly by the court cabinet-maker, Michael Kimmel or Kümmel, described in 1749 as a 'young man highly skilled in working bronze and exotic woods and experienced in the decorative French and English designs'. The cabinet was bought by Baron Mayer de Rothshild in 1835 when he was 17 years old for the large sum of £1000, and remained at the family seat of Mentmore Towers until 1977.

From the late 1760s the French porcelain factory at Sèvres began to dominate the European market for luxury ceramics. This **vase (21)** is embellished with delicately painted panels set against the rich background colour known as *bleu nouveau*. The intimate view of Jupiter embracing his lover Callisto is adapted from an engraving after the celebrated French artist François Boucher (1703-70), whose sensuous paintings were often reproduced on Sèvres porcelain. The vase was probably presented as a diplomatic gift by Louis XVI of France to Tipu Sultan, the ruler of the Indian state of Mysore, in 1788. It seems to have come to Britain after Seringapatam, Mysore's capital, was taken by the British in 1799. Tipu Sultan was killed during the long and bloody siege. The vase entered the Museum as part of the Jones Bequest in 1882. John Jones, having made his fortune as a military tailor in the Crimean war, spent some

£250,000 on a vast collection of eighteenth-century Continental decorative art which he left to the V&A. The collection's holdings of Sèvres porcelain are particularly strong, and this vase is one of the finest and most impressive examples.

20. Augustus III's writing cabinet
Europe 1600-1800, Room 5c
◄◄ W.63-1970

21. Sèvres vase
Europe 1600-1800, Room 7e
▼ 747-1882

The V&A was founded with the profits of the Great Exhibition of 1851, and many of the objects exhibited there were bought by the British Government to form the basis of the new institution's collection. This magnificent German **sideboard (22)**, designed by Ferdinand Rothbart (1823-99) and made by Thomas Hoffmeister and Thomas Behrens, was displayed in the Great Exhibition's Crystal Palace in 1851 but, unlike other objects, did not enter the Museum's collections until 1967. Instead, after the Exhibition, Kaiser Franz Joseph I of Austria presented the sideboard to Queen Victoria and Prince Albert. This was an appropriate gesture as the furniture was made in Coburg and Prince Albert was a member of the house of Saxe-Coburg. The furniture was used first in Buckingham Palace and later at Holyrood House, the monarch's official Scottish residence. This piece of furniture is designed in a

22. Oak sideboard
Europe and America
1800-1890, Room 8
W.11-1967

style known as Gothic Revival. During the nineteenth century the heavily carved decoration of the Middle Ages inspired many British and northern European designers. The Gothic was believed to be more native to their homelands than the imported classical styles of ancient Greece and Rome that had dominated much eighteenth-century design.

While the art of the past inspired the making of this latter piece of furniture, it was the art of another culture, Japan, that was admired by the French painter and graphic artist Henri de Toulouse-Lautrec (1864-1901). *Eldorado... Aristide Bruant dans son cabaret* (**23**) is one of three posters Lautrec designed for Aristide Bruant in 1892. All three show the

singer and cabaret owner, who specialized in the biting delivery of topical songs, as a powerful, almost menacing figure. The poster makes its impact through the apparent simplicity of composition, its bold outlines and solid blocks of colour which recall the style of Japanese prints. The lettering, and even the artist's monogram, form part of the overall design. Lautrec always paid meticulous attention to the processes involved in printing his posters. He worked on the lithograph stone himself, splattering colour on with the aid of a toothbrush to achieve a tonal effect, and mixing inks with a spatula to ensure the pigments were exactly those required. His interest in colour lithography and his great skill in executing the technique were influential in elevating the poster to a major art form.

23. *Eldorado...*
Aristide Bruant dans
son Cabaret **by**
Toulouse-Lautrec
Europe and America
1800-1890, Room 9
Circ.669-1967

The Sculpture Galleries

The Sculpture Courts house the National Collection of British and Continental monumental sculpture as well as an important group of sculptor's models. One of the most famous objects on display is the sculpture of composer *George Frederick Handel* **(1685-1759) (24)** by Louis-François Roubiliac (1702-62). This sculpture was commissioned by the impresario Jonathan Tyers for his famous pleasure gardens at Vauxhall. Handel is shown in the guise of Orpheus, holding a lyre. Yet despite the classical allusion, he wears informal contemporary dress: a soft cap, a long shirt open at the neck, a full, loose gown, and slippers, one of which has been discarded and lies beneath his right foot. His pose is also casual. He is seated cross-legged with his elbow leaning on a pile of bound scores of his works, including Alexander's Feast, completed the same month as the statue was finished. The statue was unprecedented, for not only was the sitter portrayed with startling informality, but it was the first life-size marble depicting a living artist. Until this date such public statues were erected only for monarchs, noblemen or military leaders. Roubiliac was a French sculptor, but all his known surviving work was executed in England. His Handel is his earliest known independent work. When it went on display in Vauxhall gardens in 1738 it proved an immediate success, helping to establish Roubiliac as one of the leading sculptors in England.

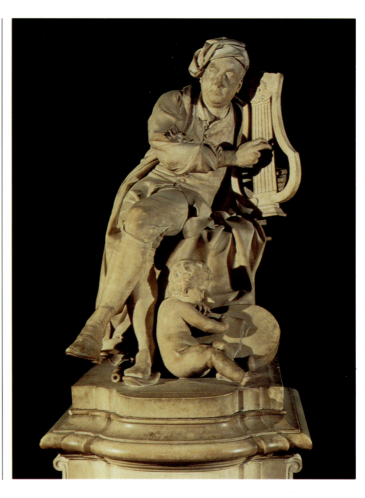

The Cast Courts

The Cast Courts **(25)** are two of the most spectacular galleries in the Museum but they do not actually contain what may be regarded as 'real' objects. Instead they are entirely devoted to reproductions. The Architectural Courts, as they were originally known, were opened in October 1873 to house the Museum's growing collection of plaster cast and electrotype reproductions. This collection was assembled for the benefit of art students who were seldom able to travel abroad to see works of art for themselves. Such educational zeal encouraged the establishment of cast collections throughout Europe, but that at the V&A is unmatched in scale and diversity and is one of the few to survive. The cast collection is valued for many reasons today, not least for the unique impression it offers of nineteenth-century ideas on museum decoration and display. This is particularly so in the atmospheric Victorian Court (46A), which has been redecorated in the original colour scheme of the 1870s. The casts also serve as precious records of many original objects which have since been damaged or destroyed.

24. *George Frederick Handel* **by Roubiliac**
Sculpture, Room 50a
A.3-1965

25. The Cast Court
Plaster casts,
Room 46a ▶

The Asian and Islamic Galleries

The Asian and Islamic Galleries display treasures from East and South-East Asia, the Indian Subcontinent, West Asia and North Africa. One of the most unusual objects on display in the **Samsung Gallery of Korean Art** is this brightly coloured **box (26)**. It is decorated with strips of painted ox-horn, a complex technique which is unique to Korea. The horn would first be soaked, flattened and then cut into thin layers. These transparent pieces would then be painted on the reverse, predominantly in red, green and yellow, before being glued to the wooden surface of the object. This box was made in about 1880-1910 and is decorated with animals and flowers. Many of these motifs carried auspicious messages: the tiger protects against evil, the tortoise represents wishes for a long life and paired birds symbolize marital harmony. The time-consuming nature of ox-horn decoration meant that boxes such as this were luxury items that only the wealthy could afford. The technique was used primarily on domestic objects made for women, such as jewellery and sewing boxes, needlecases, pillow ends and small clothes chests.

This small yet beautifully executed panel of embroidery is known as a **Rank Badge (27)** and would have served to indicate the status of a government official in Chosŏn Dynasty Korea (1392-1910). Made in the nineteenth century, it shows a pair of leopards, and

27. Rank badge
Samsung Gallery of Korean Art
FE.272-1995 ▶

26. Ox-horn box
Samsung Gallery of Korean Art
W.38-1920

would have been worn by a military official from the first to third ranks. Leopards and tigers, respected for their strength and courage in Korea, were used for the dress of military officials while civil officials wore crane motifs. This badge shows the distinctively spotted animals among rocks, waves and clouds in a pattern which remained virtually unchanged for 300 years.

The green-glazed ceramics of the Koryŏ Dynasty (935-1392) have always been greatly admired, both in Korea and abroad. These elegant and highly refined *celadons*, as this type of green ware is called, were made for use at Court and by the aristocracy. The V&A is fortunate to have many beautiful examples in its collection, including this **ewer and ritual vessel (28)**. Archaeology has often played an important part in our understanding of Asian art, and much of the interest shown in Koryŏ *celadons* in the early decades of this century resulted from the excavation of Korean tombs. The acquisitions made by the Museum at this time came from the collections of diplomats and missionaries resident in Korea, as well as from rare and discerning visitors to the country. Two such visitors were Aubrey Le Blond and his wife, who travelled to Korea in 1913-4. Their collection, which included this ewer in the form of a bamboo shoot, was given to the Museum in 1918.

At the centre of the **Gerard Godfrey Gallery of Chinese Export Art** is a magnificent model of a **pagoda (29)**. Made of seventeen tiers of porcelain, it stands over 2.7 metres (9 feet) high. Models in porcelain of this size and quality are extremely rare, and this pagoda is one of only ten that are known to exist. European trade with China reached its peak between the years of 1720 and 1840. Silks, spices, tea, porcelain and other craft items were shipped to Europe via the great port city of

Canton on China's southern coast. While most goods were produced in bulk to satisfy the growing western mass-market, objects such as this pagoda would have been made to special order. Made in about 1800-15, it is modelled on a real pagoda built in Nanking during the fifteenth century and destroyed in 1853. Such accurate sources mattered little to European customers, however. For its purchaser the pagoda would have inspired a very western vision of the mysteries of the exotic East.

28. *Celadon* **ewer and ritual vessel**
Samsung Gallery of Korean Art
C.527-1918 and C.743-1909

29. Porcelain pagoda
Gerard Godfrey Gallery of Chinese Export Art
C.80-1954 ▶

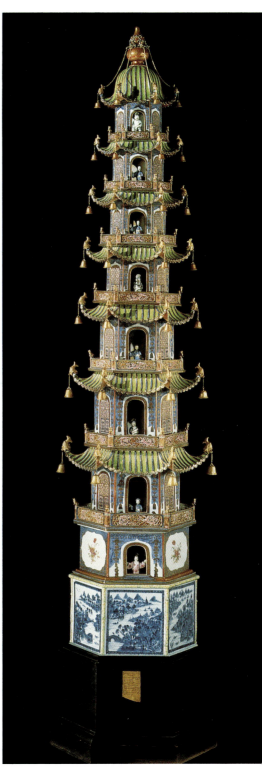

Another object made specifically for export to Europe is this **Japanese screen (30)**, which is on display in the **Toshiba Gallery of Japanese Art**. Made in the late seventeenth century, the screen is decorated with mountainous landscape scenes, pavilions, birds, animals and figures. Japanese export items began to reach Europe in the 1560s, following the arrival in Japan first of the Portuguese and then of the Dutch. Export lacquerwares were highly prized by the few Europeans who could afford to buy them. This screen is thought to have come from the collection at Hamilton Palace, which included many pieces previously owned by William Beckford (1760-1844). Aside from his fame as a novelist, Beckford was one of the most prolific European collectors of Japanese lacquer. It is unusual for such an object to have survived intact, as the practice of cutting up lacquer panels to be incorporated into pieces of furniture was widespread in eighteenth-century Europe.

30. Lacquer Japanese screen
Toshiba Gallery of
Japanese Art
FE.50-1980

No country has elevated the making of swords to such a distinguished art form as Japan. Deadly but beautiful, Japanese swords are regarded with reverence by collectors both in Japan and abroad. This **sword (31)**, which has a fourteenth-century blade and sumptuously decorated nineteenth-century mountings, belonged to Sir Harry Parkes (1828-85), the British Minister to Japan from 1865 to 1883. For a foreigner to be presented with a sword was an enormous honour. Sir Harry received his from the hands of the Meiji Emperor himself (reigned 1868-1912). It was thought that the presentation was during his first audience with the Emperor in 1868 (an occasion marked by an attack on the British delegation as it was making its way to the Imperial Palace in Kyoto by members of an anti-foreign group). However, recent research on the inscription of the swordguard, or *tsuba*, has revealed a date of 1871, indicating that the sword must have been given to Sir Harry at a later audience.

The V&A has a wonderful collection of over 20,000 Japanese woodblock prints. These prints are known as *ukiyo-e* which means 'pictures of the floating world'. In the Edo period (1615-1868), this term referred to the exciting and ever-changing delights of modern life. The prints provided popular mementos of this world, depicting in particular the famous actors and courtesans of the pleasure districts. In the nineteenth century, the range of subject matter broadened to include landscapes and legendary stories. Utagawa Kuniyoshi (1798-1861), the artist of the **print (32)** illustrated here, is especially renowned for his depictions of historical and mythical scenes. This print portrays the tenth-century witch, Takiyasha, calling up a monstrous skeleton-spectre. Because of their sensitivity to light, woodblock prints cannot be displayed for long periods of time, so the display in the Toshiba Gallery is regularly changed.

31. Mounted sword
Toshiba Gallery of
Japanese Art
M.13-1949

32. *Takiyasha the Witch and the Skeleton Spectre* by Kuniyoshi
Toshiba Gallery of
Japanese Art
E.1333-1922 ▶

The rich colours of sumptuous silk *kimono* can fade if exposed to strong light for too long so, as with the prints, the display in the Toshiba Gallery is periodically rotated. *Kimono*, which translates as 'the thing worn', were the standard item of dress for all classes and both sexes in the Edo period (1615-1868). Garments with very long sleeves, such as those on the eighteenth-century **kimono** (33) illustrated here, are known as *furisode* or 'swinging sleeves' and were worn by unmarried women. Red, regarded as a very glamorous colour, was also worn by young women. The red of this *kimono* derives from safflower, which was one of the most expensive of all dyes. *Kimono* are patterned with embroidery or by resist-dyeing techniques, the latter method used in this example being known as *shibori*. This involves the binding of small areas of the fabric so that they remain unaffected when submerged in the dye. To have a whole *kimono* patterned by this painstaking technique was extremely costly. Dress was an important

indicator of wealth, status and style in the fashion-conscious world of urban Japan, and the young woman who wore this *kimono* would certainly not have gone unnoticed.

While the majority of objects in the Toshiba Gallery reveal the artistic achievements of the past, one display highlights some of the exciting developments of the present. These striking examples of **modern Japanese ceramics, metalwork and basketry (34)** are part of a large and expanding collection of contemporary Japanese studio crafts. Raku Kichizaemon XV (b.1949) was born into a famous family of potters who have been making ceramics for the tea ceremony since the sixteenth century. While his stoneware teabowl is inspired by traditional Japanese models, the basket of cypress shavings by Sekijima Hisako (b.1944) and the copper vase covered in gold leaf by Hiramatsu Yasuki (b.1926) are more experimental in style.

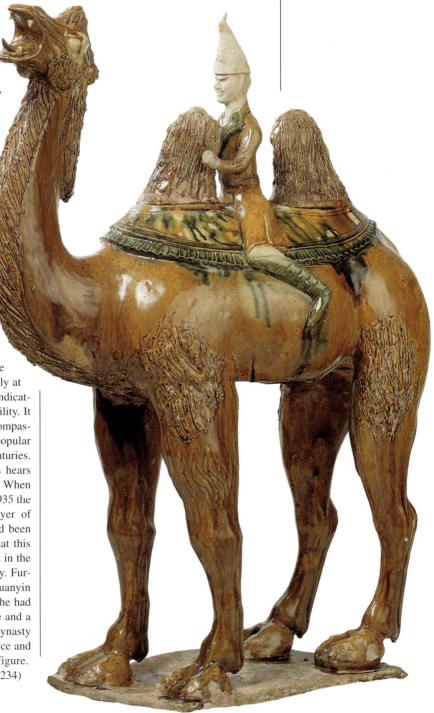

asterpieces from one of the world's greatest and most ancient cultures are on display in the **T.T. Tsui Gallery of Chinese Art**. This model of a **camel and rider (35)**, dating from about 700-50, is made of earthenware and coloured with the distinctive lead glazes of the Tang Dynasty (618-906). Such camels were often found in tombs laden with provisions for the dead. Lavish grave goods not only indicated the status and wealth of the person buried, but also reflected important aspects of Chinese life at this time. With the opening up of East-West trade routes, the double-humped bactrian camel became indispensable for transporting goods across the deserts of the Silk Road. Figures of camels therefore symbolized the economic and cultural exchange which flourished in the cosmopolitan atmosphere of Tang Dynasty China.

In Buddhist belief a *Bodhisattva* is a holy being who has reached the ultimate state of bliss, called *Nirvana*, but has chosen to come back into the world to help mankind. This beautifully carved image of the ***Bodhisattva Guanyin* (36)** sits completely at ease upon his rocky throne, a posture indicating both serenity and a worldly accessibility. It is this accommodating disposition and compassion that has made Guanyin such a popular figure for Chinese believers over the centuries. His name means 'the one who always hears sounds', so he will listen to every prayer. When the Museum acquired this sculpture in 1935 the whole surface was covered with a layer of paper over which paint and gilding had been applied. Conservation work revealed that this was a crude attempt at repair carried out in the late nineteenth or early twentieth century. Further research revealed that when the Guanyin was originally decorated in about 1200 he had a bright red and green skirt, a blue stole and a gold crown. Later, during the Ming Dynasty (1368-1644), the statue was repaired twice and redecorated to look like a gilt bronze figure. Little of the original Jin period (1115-1234)

decoration remains, but conservators at the Museum have been able to reveal much of the red and gold of the Ming period restorations.

35. Earthenware camel and rider
T.T. Tsui Gallery of Chinese Art
C.880-1936

36. *The Bodhisattva Guanyin*
T.T. Tsui Gallery of Chinese Art
A.7-1935

37. Lacquer table
T.T. Tsui Gallery of Chinese Art
FE.6-1973

No era of Chinese history has inspired as much fascination as the Ming Dynasty (1368-1644). This **table (37)**, unique in shape and decoration, is one of the most important objects from the period. It is one of the only surviving examples in the world of a major piece of furniture produced in the 'Orchard Workshop', the Imperial lacquer workshop set up in the early Ming period and situated to the north-west of the 'Forbidden City' compound in Peking (now Beijing). The table bears the mark of the reign of the Emperor Xuande (1426-35) and was probably made to stand in an Imperial Palace. An Imperial provenance is also suggested by the five-clawed dragons carved on the surface, each of which have been strangely mutilated by the removal of one claw on each foot.

The objects on display in the **Islamic Gallery** come from several different countries including Egypt, Turkey, Iran, Iraq and Syria. The **Ardabil Carpet (38)** is one of the largest and most magnificent Persian carpets in the world. Named after the shrine in north-west Iran in which it is said to have been used, the carpet includes an inscription which bears the Islamic date 946 AH, which is equivalent to 1539-40. The beautiful and harmonious design, and the technical virtuosity demonstrated in the weaving of a carpet 10.7 metres (35 feet) long, 5.3 metres (17^1/$_2$ feet) wide – with 76.4 kilometres (47^1/$_2$ miles) of silk warp, 124.7 kilometres (77^1/$_2$ miles) of silk weft and 29,559,600 knots – made the Ardabil Carpet a spectacular acquisition when it was bought by the Museum in 1893 for the then staggering sum of £2,000. The famous Victorian designer William Morris was one of those who recommended its purchase, stating that it was 'of singular perfection ... by far the finest Eastern carpet which I have ever seen.'

This **basin (39)** is made of brass inlaid with gold and silver. The lavish decoration includes eight medallions around the rim, depicting mounted horsemen engaged in hunting and seated figures holding crescents, symbolizing the moon. At the edge of the rim is a delicate lattice pattern of ducks, while the flat base has panels showing musicians. On the side are inscriptions, written in *thuluth* script, which give the titles of the owner and invoke

38. The Ardabil Carpet
Islamic Galleries, Room 42
◀ 272-1893

40. Rock crystal ewer
Islamic Galleries, Room 42
7904-1862 ▶

39. Inlaid brass basin
Islamic Galleries, Room 42
▼ 740-1898

his glory and prosperity. The basin was made in Egypt or Syria in about 1300, and is one of a group of similar objects which were probably used for ritual washing. Many bear the titles of well-known rulers, but the identity of the owner of this example remains a mystery. Although he may not have been of royal blood, there is no doubt that he was wealthy enough to employ the most superior craftsmen.

Carved from a single block of rock crystal, this **ewer (40)** is a work of outstanding quality. Made in Egypt in the late tenth century, it is exquisitely decorated with fantastic birds, beasts and twisting tendrils. The Treasure of Caliph Mostansir-Billah at Cairo, which was destroyed in 1062, apparently contained 1,800 rock crystal vessels. Only a few of these have survived to bear witness to the splendour of the Egyptian caliphs, this example being one of the finest.

Tilework has traditionally played a major role in Ottoman architecture, adding vibrant splashes of colour to buildings of monumental grandeur. One of the most important centres for tile-making was Iznik in Turkey. It was here in the late sixteenth century that the most brilliant tiles were produced to adorn the many new buildings being erected in nearby Istanbul, the capital of the Ottoman Empire. By the early eighteenth century the industry at Iznik had all but died out. However, one group of skilled craftsmen moved to Istanbul and established the Tekfur Saray factory, producing tiles that revived earlier styles. It was here, in 1731, that this **magnificent fireplace (41)** was made. It originally stood in the Palace of Fuad Pacha, until this was destroyed in Istanbul's great fire of 1857. This fireplace is an important example of the Museum's incomparable collection of Islamic tilework and pottery.

Indian sculpture is an art created in the service of religion. The Buddhist, Jain and Hindu images were created both to honour the deity represented and to be a means by which the faithful, through ritual and prayer, could seek protection and benevolence. No stylistic distinctions were made between sculptures made for the different sects, the deities being identifiable from their form and the attributes they carry. This gilt copper sculpture shows *The Buddha* **(42)** dressed in the robes of a monk, his right hand raised in a gesture of reassurance to the faithful. His extended earlobes, the flame motif on his skull and the auspicious forehead mark identify him as the enlightened Prince

41. Tiled fireplace
Islamic Galleries,
Room 47c
◄ 703-1891

43. *Jina Parshvanatha*
Indian Sculpture,
Room 47b
931(IS) ►

▲
42. *The Buddha*
Indian Sculpture,
Room 47b
IPN.2639

Shakyamuni. He stands on a double lotus flower, the Buddhist symbol of purity. This sculpture is one of the finest Buddhist metal sculptures to survive from southern India. It dates from the eleventh or twelfth century when the region was an important seat of Buddhist learning. Centres such as the port-city of Nagapattinam, the most likely source of this image, received royal endowments not only from the local Chola dynasty but also from the Buddhist rulers of overseas kingdoms, such as the Sailendra of Java. Generous patronage from both royal and private donors provided for the creation of many images of the Buddha, but few surpass the calm majesty and authority of this figure.

Jainism is the least well known of India's ancient religions, with a history reaching back beyond Buddhism to at least 700 BC. This sculpture depicts one of the 24 Jina, or 'liberated souls', of the religion, the 23rd *Jina Parshvanatha* **(43)**. Jina images are represented either seated in meditation or, as here, standing in a posture of abandoning the body, an act of severe penance undertaken on the path to spiritual liberation. This image of Parshvanatha dates from the twelfth or thirteenth century and belongs to the *Digambara*, or 'sky-clad' sect of Jainism, whose ascetic followers renounce all worldly possessions. With his multi-headed snake canopy, Parshvanatha is the most readily identified of the 24 Jinas. This imagery derives from the Jain legend of the serpent king Dharana, who protected the Jina with the coils of his body and sheltered him with his seven-headed hood. On the base of the sculpture is an inscription recording that it was commissioned as part of the renovation of a Jain temple at Yalburga in Karnataka, southern India, in the reign of one Mummudi Singa. The names of the sponsor and the sculptor are recorded, the latter a rare occurrence in Indian art.

44. *Shiva Nataraja, the Lord of the Dance*
Indian Sculpture,
Room 47b
IM.2-1934

45. Page from the
Akbarnama
Nehru Gallery of
Indian Art
IS.2-1896 ▶

This sculpture, made in Tamilnadu, southern India, in about 900, shows the Hindu deity *Shiva* (**44**) performing the *nadanta* dance through which the elemental forces of the universe are cyclically created, maintained and destroyed. Ringed by a circle of flames, Shiva dances on the back of the prostrate dwarf Apasmara, who signifies the power of ignorance and materialism. In his upper hands Shiva holds a drum and a tongue of flame, which symbolize the complementary universal principles of Creation and Destruction, while with his lower hands he offers protection and the possibility of salvation. Much of our knowledge of the meaning of gestures in Indian sculpture comes from the language of movement in Indian sacred dance. The posture assumed by Shiva Nataraja in this image is borrowed directly from temple dance. The rings around the base of the sculpture would have been used to secure the image during processions. On such occasions, which form an important part of the ritual life of a Hindu temple, portable images of the presiding deity are bathed and suitably dressed before being carried around the temple grounds on special platforms.

Sculpture forms only one part of the Museum's extensive collection of Indian art, which is unrivalled outside the Indian subcontinent. Other highlights from the collection are displayed in the **Nehru Gallery of Indian Art**. Some of the most spectacular artistic achievements date from the period of the Mughal Empire, which was established in 1526 by Zahir ad-Din Muhammad Babur. His grandson Akbar became ruler of India in 1556 at the age of 13. By the end of the sixteenth century Akbar had created a stable empire and was able to concentrate on artistic projects, such as commissioning illustrated books like the *Akbarnama* (**45**). This history of his reign was written in Persian, the language of the court, by the historian Abul Fazl in about 1590. The surviving section of the royal copy in the V&A includes amongst its pages 116 miniatures painted by Akbar's finest artists, and depicts gory battle-scenes as well as major events at court such as the arrival of foreign ambassadors or the construction of new monuments. Each page was usually the work of two artists, the first being responsible for the composition and the second, more junior artist, for the painting. On some pages a third, specialist artist added the faces of the more important figures. These paintings are very sensitive to light and the pages of the *Akbarnama* displayed in the Nehru Gallery are regularly changed.

Akbar's grandson, Shah Jahan, was the fifth Mughal emperor of India. He was an important patron of architecture and is famous for building the Taj Mahal. He was also a connoisseur of precious and semi-precious stones. Some of the most important surviving Mughal jades, of which this **wine cup (46)** is arguably the finest, were made for or were owned by him. A lightly incised inscription records that the cup was completed for the Emperor in the thirty-first year of his reign, in the year 1067 of the Islamic calendar, equivalent to 1657. It was in this year that Shah Jahan was deposed and imprisoned by his son Aurangzeb, who then took the throne.

Textiles have played an important part in India's cultural history and the V&A's superb collection numbers over 10,000 pieces, which are displayed on a changing basis. Illustrated here is an exquisitely painted small cotton **coverlet (47)**. The design is heavily indebted to Iranian painting traditions, with nobles in Persian dress interspersed with more typically Indian figures. The coverlet was made in Golconda in south-east India in about 1625-50. This region was pre-eminent in the complicated dyeing techniques that made Indian textiles so highly prized. It was this type of painted textile that initially attracted the attention of the British East India Company, who started importing Indian textiles into Europe in the early seven-

47. Cotton coverlet
Nehru Gallery of
Indian Art
IS.34-1969 ▶

46. Shah Jahan's wine cup
Nehru Gallery of
Indian Art
▼ IS.12-1962

teenth century. The designs were adapted to suit European taste, and evolved into painted cottons known as chintz.

With the collapse of the Mughal Empire in the eighteenth century, the East India Company began to acquire more political and military control of India. These dazzling **turban jewels (48)** were presented to Admiral Charles Watson by the Nawab of Bengal, Mir Ja'far Ali Khan, on 26 July 1757 after the battle of Plassey. This was fought, under the overall

48. Turban jewels
Nehru Gallery of
Indian Art
IS.3-1982

49. *Tippoo's Tiger*
Nehru Gallery of
Indian Art
2545(IS) ▶

and Watson. Made of enamelled gold set with diamonds, rubies, emeralds, a sapphire and a pendant pearl, Watson's jewels are typical of those worn at the court in Murshidabad in this period. They remained in the possession of his descendants until 1982, when the Museum bought them at auction, and are extremely rare examples of documented eighteenth-century Indian jewellery.

Under the rule of Haidar Ali Khan and his son, Tipu Sultan, the state of Mysore was the greatest threat to the authority of the East India Company in southern India in the late eighteenth century. Tipu's military prowess and his adoption of the tiger as his personal symbol earned him the title 'Tiger of Mysore'. Tiger motifs adorned many of his possessions, from his throne to his weaponry. This extraordinary **model of a tiger devouring a man (49)** reveals Tipu's fascination with new technologies and may have been inspired by the gruesome fate that befell the son of an old adversary, General Sir Hector Munro, in Bengal. The tiger's body contains an organ which ingeniously simulates its growls and the shrieks of its victim. Brought to London after Tipu's defeat at Seringapatam in 1799, this object became the most famous exhibit in the East India Company's Museum. Much of the Company's collection was later transferred to the V&A where 'Tippoo's Tiger' continues to be a favourite with visitors.

command of Robert Clive, in order to protect British trading interests in Bengal by deposing the legitimate ruler, Siraj ad-Daula, and replacing him with Mir Ja'far. When the new Nawab was safely installed he gave presents to Clive

Ranjit Singh, known by the British as the 'Lion of the Punjab', was an outstanding ruler who reconciled the warring factions of the region to create a powerful and stable Sikh nation. He became Maharaja in 1801 and was renowned for the simplicity of his appearance and dislike of ceremony. This probably means that he sat on this **golden throne (50)** only rarely, preferring to sit cross-legged on carpets. Paradoxically his court was one of the most splendid in the subcontinent, and his many European visitors left vivid accounts of his richly bejewelled military chiefs, the massive emeralds and diamonds that decorated his horses and the expensive Kashmir shawls that lined his tents. The throne was part of the State Property taken by the British in 1849 on the annexation of the Punjab, and was displayed with other treasures of the Indian Empire at the Great Exhibition in 1851.

50. The throne of Maharaja Ranjit Singh
Nehru Gallery of Indian Art
2518(IS)

The production of art in **Nepal** was largely confined to the Newars who, although mainly Buddhists themselves, were responsible for the religious art of both Hindu and Buddhist communities alike. The unsurpassed metal-working skills of the Newari community are evident in these sixteenth-century **reliefs (51)**. These would once have formed the central section of a decorative panel mounted above the entrance to a Hindu temple or the private enclosure of a domestic shrine. The central motif is Garuda, the mythical bird who attends the Hindu deity Vishnu and serves as his sacred vehicle. Garuda is seen with spread wings, his extended talons clasping his enemies: the snake-spirits *nāga* and *nāginī*. This kind of metal decoration is known as *repoussé* and is produced by hammering from the inside. The highly raised copper forms of these reliefs are mercury gilded and set with rock crystal, turquoise and semi-precious stones, to achieve an effect of great opulence and splendour.

South-East Asia encompasses the states of Burma, Thailand, Laos, Vietnam, Cambodia, Malaysia, Indonesia and the Philippines. This region gained much of its wealth as a trading centre serving the great East-West trade routes which linked China with India and the Near East. This **container (52)**, of embossed gold and filigree work set with rubies and emeralds, was made in Burma (now Myanmar), in the nineteenth century. It was designed to hold betel, a mild narcotic chewed throughout Asia and traditionally made from areca nuts and lime wrapped in a betel leaf. The container is in the form of a mythical bird known as a *karaweik*. This has been an important motif in Burmese art since the seventh century, and was believed to possess the ideal Buddhist qualities of purity and gentleness. Although containers in this form are common enough in Myanmar, this particular object is of great historical significance since it formed part of the Burmese regalia used by the last king, Thi-baw Min. The regalia were requisitioned by the British as indemnity at the end of the Third Burmese War in 1885 and remained under the custodianship of the V&A from 1886 until 1964, when they were returned to Myanmar. This container was given to the Museum by the Government and people of Myanmar in recognition of its care of the regalia.

51. Gateway reliefs
South East Asia and the Himalayas, Room 47a
IM.142-1926

52. Betel container in the form of a sacred bird
South East Asia and the Himalayas, Room 47a
IS.246-1964

The Raphael Gallery

The **Raphael Gallery** houses the surviving designs by Raphael (1483-1520) for tapestries commissioned in 1515 by Pope Leo X for the Sistine Chapel in the Vatican. Raphael was a younger contemporary of both Leonardo da Vinci and Michelangelo, and these designs are among the greatest works of art to have survived from the period of the High Renaissance. The designs are also known as 'cartoons' after the Italian word *cartone*, meaning a large piece of paper. The cartoons were cut into strips to enable the weavers to use them as guides for each section of the tapestry. It was not until 1699 that the strips were stuck together and mounted on canvas. The subject of the cartoons are taken from the lives of St Peter and St Paul. ***Christ's Charge to Peter*** (53) combines two incidents from the gospels, one in which Christ instructs Peter to 'Feed my Sheep', and another in which he gives him the keys to heaven.

The seven cartoons, which rank amongst the greatest artistic treasures in Britain, have belonged to the Royal Family since 1623. They have been on loan to the Museum since 1865.

53. ***Christ's Charge to Peter*** **by Raphael**
Raphael Gallery, Room 48a

The Dress Gallery

54. Embroidered jacket and companion portrait of Margaret Laton
Dress Gallery, Room 40
T.228-1994 and E.214-1994

The Dress Gallery covers over 400 years of European fashionable dress from the mid-sixteenth century to the present day. This early seventeenth-century **embroidered jacket and its companion portrait (54)** are unique, for although jackets and contemporary portraits showing women wearing such items do exist, there are no other known 'paired' survivals of this kind. The jacket was originally owned and worn by Margaret Laton (1579-1641) wife of Francis Laton (1577-1661), who was one of the Yeomen of the Jewel House during the reigns of James I, Charles I and, briefly, Charles II.

Embroidered linen jackets were worn as informal dress, and were particularly popular among wealthy women in the late sixteenth and early seventeenth centuries. This jacket is exquisitely decorated with flowers, birds and butterflies embroidered in coloured silks, coiled tendrils of silver-gilt plaited braid stitch and silver-gilt sequins. The edges of the jacket are trimmed with silver and silver-gilt bobbin lace and silver-gilt spangles. The portrait showing Margaret Laton wearing the jacket is painted in oils on oak boards and probably dates from around 1620. The painter is not known, but the style of portraiture is similar to that of Marcus Gheeraerts the Younger (1561?-1635) who was the most fashionable portrait painter of the period.

This splendid **suit (55)** was worn by James, Duke of York (1633-1701), later King James II (reigned 1685-8), at the ceremony confirming his marriage contract in 1673 to Mary Beatrice d'Este, daughter of the Duke of Modena. The suit was presented as a gift to Sir Edward Carteret who attended the ceremony. After Sir Edward's death it passed to the de Sausmarez family and continued by descent in this family until it was acquired by the V&A in 1995. It is exceedingly unusual for such an important outfit, firmly associated with the British Royal family, to have survived unscathed for over three hundred years. The suit is made of wool and embroidered in silver and silver-gilt thread. It is a rare example of a transitional style of dress, showing the fitted coat being worn with full-cut breeches. These replaced the antique stiffened doublet and petticoat breeches of the 1650s and 1660s. James's extravagantly wide breeches have deep turned-up cuffs, held in place by a series of silver-gilt looped cords and buttons.

The **mantua (56)** was a robe worn open over a petticoat, the latter being designed for show rather than as an undergarment. First developed as a loose, informal 'undress' gown in the 1670s, by the 1740s it had a highly structured shape and was the customary formal dress worn for court or ceremonial occasions. In the eighteenth century, the mantua was worn over wide side-hoops, or *paniers*, which reached their most extraordinary proportions in the 1740s. The petticoat of this outfit is made up of seven widths of silk and fits a flexible hooped under-petticoat which, at its maximum, is 1.5 metres (5 feet) wide. Even by 1710, satirists were poking fun at these amazing garments. In 1713 it was commented that a lady who had fallen over looked like 'an over-turned bell without a clapper'. This elaborately embroidered dress is believed to have been worn by Isabella Courtenay at her wedding in Exeter Cathedral on 14 May 1744.

55. James II's wedding suit
Dress Gallery, Room 40
T.771-1995

Also on display in the Dress Gallery are fashion accessories such as shoes, hats and fans. This green silk **brisé fan (57)** is Italian and, dating from about 1620-40, is the earliest example in the Museum's collection. Fans were made in Japan and China from the tenth century AD, but did not reach Europe until the second half of the sixteenth century.

The term *brisé* describes a fan made entirely with decorated sticks, without a fan 'leaf'. The individual sticks of this fan are shaped to imitate feathers, and the decoration, in delicate straw appliqué work, is of exotic birds and flowers. In the early seventeenth century straw-work of this high quality was produced in the area around Florence. Both *brisé* fans and fans with folding leaves were popular in the late sixteenth and early seventeenth centuries. Although many portraits of this period show fans being held in the hand, very few have survived.

56. Embroidered mantua
Dress Gallery,
Room 40
◀ T.260-1969

57. Brisé fan
Dress Gallery,
Room 40
▲ T.184-1982

This **evening dress (58)**, of satin, chiffon and velvet, is by Lucile (Lady Duff Gordon) (1862-1935). The sister of novelist Elinor Glyn, Lucile was a self-taught designer and opened her first shop in Burlington Street, London, in 1895. She quickly gained a reputation for her romantic tea gowns and fairytale, special-occasion dresses and, at her peak, had branches in New York and Paris. She also designed theatrical costumes. Lucile was much inspired by historical styles, especially those of the eighteenth and nineteenth centuries. This dress, of about 1912-13, is one of her more restrained designs. It is cut in the high-waisted style known as 'Directoire' which was fashionable from the 1790s to 1810. A woman of Bohemian leanings, Lucile was considered very 'racy' in her day and was one of the first designers to show her clothes on live models, which created a great stir.

Shown at Christian Dior's first, seminal collection of spring 1947, the **Bar suit (59)** was one of the most popular of the designs that came to be known as the 'New Look'. In complete contrast to the austere designs of the war years, Dior employed lavish quantities of the finest fabrics and a complex inner construction to achieve this exaggeratedly shapely style. The cream silk jacket is cut to fit tightly above the narrow, 46-centimetre (18-inch) waist, while below it has a deep basque which is stiffened, padded and weighted to create 'teacup' curves over the hips. The black wool crepe skirt is very full, measuring 7.3 metres (24 feet) around the hem. This dramatic new style received mixed responses. Government officials were scandalized by what they considered to be a waste of scarce resources, and some women complained that it was anachronistic. Most women loved it, however, and soon adopted modified versions.

Since his first show in 1971, Issey Miyake (b.1935) has become an innovative fashion force, fusing elements from the traditional designs of his native Japan with uncompromising modernity. His clothes are admired for their deceptive simplicity and wearability as well as

58. Evening dress by Lucile
Dress Gallery, Room 40
◀ T.31-1960

59. *Bar* Suit by Dior
Dress Gallery, Room 40
◄ T.376 and 377-1960

**60. *Rhythm Pleats*
dress by Miyake**
Dress Gallery, Room 40
T.231-1992 ►

for their more formal sculptural qualities. This **dress (60)** is from his 1990 'Rhythm Pleats' collection. Here Miyake has created two- and three-dimensional shapes through geometric cutting and the exploitation of the linear qualities of the pleats, which are often placed at different angles. The garment is designed to move with the wearer, assuming independent forms which neither disguise nor reveal the body. Miyake displayed his 1990 collection in an influential exhibition in which dresses were shown on three-dimensional mannequins as well as spread flat on the floor. This dress has a rectangular shape when laid out flat.

The British Galleries

The **British Galleries** house the Museum's outstanding collection of art from the Tudor, Stuart, Georgian and Victorian periods. Henry VIII, who became king in 1509, was a great patron of the arts. Many of the luxury objects made for him and his court show the influence of new ideas from Renaissance Europe. This portable **writing desk (61)**, made in about 1525-6, was probably used by the king and is lavishly embellished with ornamental motifs introduced to Britain by Continental artists. The gilded leather lining is painted with figures and profile heads that are close in style to contemporary portrait miniatures by Lucas Hornebolte (c.1490-1544), an artist from Ghent, while the figures of Mars in armour and Venus with Cupid are taken from woodcuts by the German artist Hans Burgkmair (1473-1531). The desk also bears the coat-of-arms and personal badges of Henry VIII and his first queen, Catherine of Aragon. Such images conveyed powerful messages of ownership and allegiance, and were used extensively in the decorative schemes of Henry VIII's royal palaces. The Latin inscription on the inner lid reads 'God of Kingdoms great Protector of the authority of the Christian Church give to your servant Henry VIII King of England a great victory over his enemies'.

This richly mounted **cup (62)**, crowned with St George slaying the Dragon, is another rare survivor from the Tudor Court. The ivory bowl is said to have belonged to Sir Thomas à Becket, Archbishop of Canterbury, who was murdered in his Cathedral in 1170. Such relics of England's favourite saint were treasured until the Reformation. When the gilded silver mounts were commissioned in 1525, the engraver was instructed to incorporate the initials TB and a mitre, in reference to the Becket association, on the cover. These alternate with the pomegranate badge of Catherine of Aragon, suggesting that the queen herself may have ordered the cup. The vital role played by prints in the dis-

semination of Renaissance styles to northern Europe is revealed in some of the ornamentation on the cup which, like the writing box, derives from the work of Hans Burgkmair. The cast marks and sheaves taken from an engraving by the artist are the earliest example of Renaissance influence in English goldsmiths' work. Later owned by Henry Howard, Earl of Northampton (d.1614), the cup descended in the Howard family, renowned both as devout Roman Catholics and as art collectors, until it was bought by the Museum in 1931.

61. Henry VIII's writing desk
Britain 1500-1750
Room 52
W.29-1932

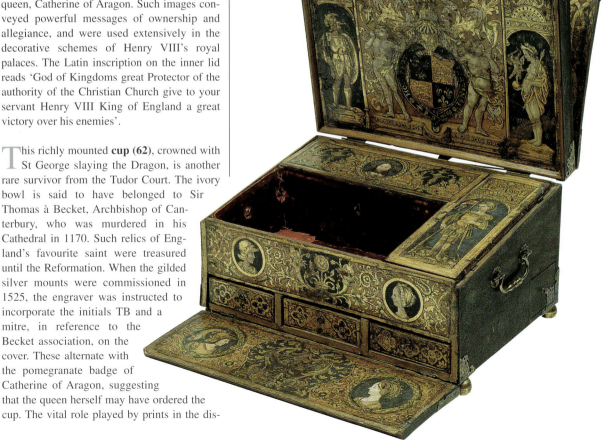

62. The Howard Grace cup
Britain 1500-1750, Room 52
◀ M.2680-1931

63. Embroidered velvet mittens
Britain 1500-1750, Room 53
1507-1882 ▶

needlework was done domestically in this period. Queen Elizabeth I and Mary Queen of Scots both embroidered for their own pleasure. The superb quality of the work on these mittens suggests, however, that they were made professionally.

This beautiful **pair of mittens (63)**, made between 1580 and 1600, also have royal connections. They are believed to have been a gift from Queen Elizabeth I to her Maid of Honour, Margaret Edgcumbe. Elaborately embroidered gloves were often given as presents in the Elizabethan period, as a sign of respect or gratitude. Their gorgeous but impractical decoration suggests they were intended to confer status rather than to be used, and they can be seen in many portraits of the period, held in the hand. They were usually made of fine leather, with silk gauntlets, and contemporary references record they were frequently 'perfumed'. Mittens of velvet such as these are very unusual. Much intricate and decorative

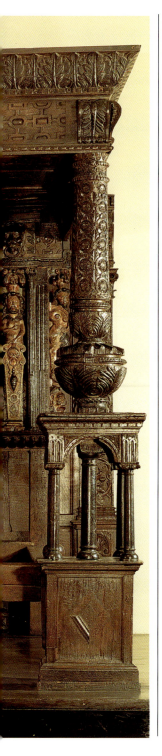

**64. The Great Bed
of Ware**
Britain 1500-1750,
Room 54
◄ W.47-1931

**65. John Evelyn's
cabinet**
Britain 1500-1750,
Room 55
W.24-1977 ►

The Great Bed of Ware (64) is the most celebrated piece of English furniture in the world. Like many objects made at the time, the bed is carved with patterns derived from European Renaissance ornament. Originally it would have been brightly painted, and traces of these colours can still be seen on the underside of the tester (canopy). The design of the marquetry panels is derived from the work of Dutch artist Hans Vredeman de Vries (1527-1604), and they were probably made by German craftsmen working in London in the late Elizabethan period. The bed was made in about 1590-1600 for one of the inns in Ware, Hertfordshire, its amazing size designed to attract the attention, and therefore the custom, of those travelling to and from London. The bed achieved early fame when Shakespeare referred to it in his play *Twelfth Night*, which was first performed in 1601: Sir Toby Belch describes a sheet as 'big enough for the bed of Ware'.

This **cabinet (65)** was made for the diarist John Evelyn (1620-1706), and is an early example of a piece of furniture commissioned by a British visitor making the 'Grand Tour' of Europe. The cabinet itself is probably French and was made to incorporate the *pietre dure*, or 'hard stone', panels which Evelyn had purchased from their maker, Domenico Benotti, in Florence in 1644. The cabinet was then extended to accommodate the bronze reliefs which show Orpheus singing to the beasts. The manuscript of Evelyn's diary was first published in the early nineteenth century, long after his death. The national recognition he achieved in turn gave the cabinet new significance' and it was further enlarged and embellished. Objects often acquire their fame because of who owned them; what makes this cabinet so fascinating is that its ownership actually influenced its physical appearance.

As well as individual objects, the British Galleries contain actual rooms from several great English town and country houses. These give a wonderful sense of the original setting of many of the things on display. One of the most lavish rooms is the **Music Room from Norfolk House (66)**. The house, situated in St James's Square in London, was designed for the 9th Duke and Duchess of Norfolk by Matthew Brettingham (1725-1803). The exterior of the house was rather austere in appearance, but the interiors were sumptuous. They were the work of Giovanni Battista Borra (1712-86) who was from Piedmont in Italy. Another Continental craftsman, Frenchman Jean Cuenot (active 1744-62), was responsible for the carved panelling and mirror frames, while the trophies on the ceiling of the Music Room, representing the Arts and Sciences, are by James Lovell (active 1750-80). The combined talents of these craftsmen were admired by Horace Walpole

66. The Music Room from Norfolk House
Britain 1500-1750,
Room 58
W.70-1938

(1718-97) who attended the grand opening of Norfolk House in February 1756, noting that 'the illumination, the glasses, the lightness and novelty of the ornaments and the ceilings are delightful'.

Although contemporary with the classically inspired interior of Norfolk House, the setting for which this extraordinary **bed (67)** was made could not have been more different. It was commissioned by the 4th Duke and Duchess of Beaufort for the Chinese Bedroom at Badminton House, Gloucestershire. From the early seventeenth century, the European fascination with objects imported from China by the Dutch and British East India Companies inspired European designers and craftsmen to imitate and create their own extremely fanciful visions of the East. The bed was part of a suite of furniture designed in this *chinoiserie* style by William (*c*.1703-63) and John (1729-96) Linnell in about 1754. It has a pagoda-like canopy, embellished with dragons, and retains much of its original japanned (imitation lacquer) surface of red, blue and gold, although the yellow silk hangings are modern copies. By the mid-eighteenth century the taste for exotic Chinese style furnishings was particularly seen in the decoration of ladies' bedrooms and dressing rooms.

67. The Badminton Bed
Britain 1750-1900,
Room 125
W.143-1921 ▶

This grand **tea and coffee service (69)**, designed in the most stylish neoclassical taste, shows that in eighteenth-century English society serving tea to company was an opportunity for the display of status and wealth. The silver bears the armorials of the renowned actor-manager David Garrick (1717-79) and his wife Eva Maria Veigel. Regarded by some of their contemporaries as social climbers, the Garricks were nevertheless part of literary, artistic and aristocratic circles, where fashionable clothing and furnishing were essential to credibility. A surviving bill reveals that the service cost the rather large sum of £88 14s. It was made in 1774-5 and may well have been commissioned for the Garrick's new home in the Adelphi, which was designed by the famous architect Robert Adam (1728-92). The ceiling from the drawing room, in which the tea and coffee service could well have been used, was saved before the demolition of the Adelphi and is displayed nearby.

68. Copy of the Portland vase by Wedgwood
Britain 1750-1900, Room 123
◄ 2418-1901

69. Part of Garrick's tea and coffee service
Britain 1750-1900, Room 122
▼ M.74-1973

The most celebrated work of Josiah Wedgwood (1730-95), the great Staffordshire potter and pioneer industrialist, was his copy of the **Portland Vase (68)**. The original cameo cut-glass vase was made in about 30-20 BC and, at the time that Wedgwood was working, was the most famous artefact to have survived from ancient Rome. The sculptor John Flaxman (1755-1826) described it enthusiastically to Wedgwood, stating that it was 'the finest production of Art that has been brought to England and seems to be the very apex of perfection to which you are endeavouring'. Wedgwood's copies of the vase were made in Jasperware, the type of refined stoneware with which his name is virtually synonymous today. His ability to use this material to recreate the subtle relief carving of the original vase was a remarkable technical achievement. Perfected in 1790, after four years of painstaking trials, the 'first edition' copies of the vase were Wedgwood's last major achievement. This particular vase is said to have come from the collection of Wedgwood's grandson, the naturalist Charles Darwin (1809-82).

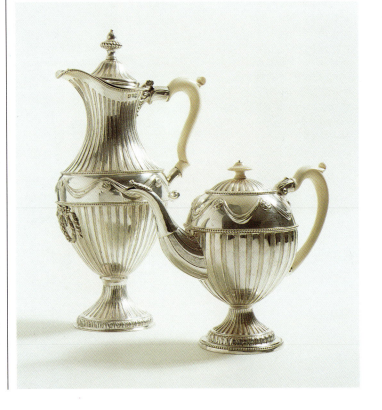

Bashaw **(71)**, a Newfoundland dog, sat some fifty times for his remarkable portrait. Bashaw's owner, Lord Dudley and Ward, commissioned the marble sculpture from Matthew Cotes Wyatt (1777-1862) in 1831. The work was to have been displayed in Lord Dudley's house in Park Lane, but he died in 1833, the year before it was finished, and *Bashaw* remained in the possession of the sculptor until his death in 1862. Dogs' portraits were occasionally painted during the nineteenth century, but this elaborate lifesize sculpted piece, originally set with gems, is unique. In 1851 it was shown at the Great Exhibition in London, where it was entitled *The Faithful Friend to Man Trampling Underfoot his Most Insidious Enemy*, the bronze boa-constrictor beneath the dog's feet symbolizing man's enemy. The placid expression of the dog, and the elegant cushion on which he stands, contrast with the coiled energy of the snake.

This amazing **vase (70)** was made at Rockingham, a ceramic factory famed for its rich and extravagant porcelains. Made in 1826, only one year after the company started to produce porcelain, this is one of a pair of colossal 'scent jars', designed to demonstrate every aspect of the factory's technical and artistic proficiency. One of the vases was displayed at the factory. The other, with its superb flower-painting by Edwin Steele, is thought to have been placed in the company's London showrooms in Piccadilly where it would have been much admired. Bought for a large sum by the Museum in 1869, the vase continues to astound, although exactly why an armour-plated rhinoceros should have been chosen for the finial on a fragile porcelain vase remains a tantalizing mystery.

Also on display at the Great Exhibition of 1851 was this **armoire (72)**, or cupboard, designed by Augustus Welby Northmore Pugin (1812-52) and made by J.G. Crace. The shields along the top and the carved decorative motifs were drawn from medieval sources. Many designers of the Victorian period were inspired by the art of the Middle Ages, but Pugin was probably the greatest and most ardent exponent of the Gothic Revival style. A prolific designer, best remembered for his decoration of the Houses of Parliament, Pugin exhausted himself and died the year after this cupboard was made. He was aged only forty. The Museum bought the cupboard directly from the 1851 Exhibition, making it one of its earliest acquisitions.

72. Armoire by Pugin
Britain 1750-1900,
Room 120
25-1852

73. Sideboard by Godwin
Britain 1750-1900, Room 119
Circ.38-1953

The stark, geometric form and unornamented surfaces of this **sideboard (73)** are so unlike the heavily decorated style of Pugin's armoire that it is difficult to believe that it was made less than twenty years later. The sideboard was designed by E.W. Godwin (1833-80) who was one of the most important exponents of Victorian 'Japonisme', the term used to describe the appreciation and appropriation of Japanese artistic styles. Japan began trading with the West in the 1850s, and by the next decade imported Japanese prints, ceramics and textiles were very fashionable in Britain. Godwin was influenced by the interiors depicted in Japanese prints and by the studies he made of Japanese architecture, but he did not seek to imitate Japanese designs. Instead, his Anglo-Japanese furniture aimed to combine the more general principles of simplicity and elegance that he admired in the art of Japan, with the domestic needs of the Victorian home.

The 20th Century Gallery

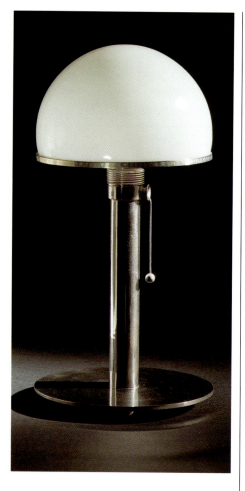

74. Table Lamp
20th Century, Room 74
◀ M.28-1989

75. The Painter-
Stainers' cup
20th Century, Room 74
M.106-1966 ▶

The **20th Century Gallery** displays some of the most significant and striking objects made between 1900 and the present day. The Bauhaus school, set up in Weimar, Germany, in 1919, had a revolutionary effect on twentieth-century design. This **table lamp (74)**, entitled *MT8*, was produced at the school in about 1924 and shows the decisive influence of the Hungarian artist, Laslo Moholy-Nagy (1895-1946). He had joined the Bauhaus as Form Master of the Metal workshop the previous year. The teaching practices of the institution were fundamentally changed by Moholy-Nagy. He transformed the Metal studio into a 'workshop of industrial design' and encouraged the students to concentrate on a geometric approach to

formal problems, and to experiment with new materials rather than adopt purely decorative solutions. Of all the designs produced by the Bauhaus few are as beautiful or emblematic of its principles as this lamp by Wilhelm Wagenfeld (1900-90). Its geometric design, subtle proportions and use of industrial materials suggest a machine age sculpture as much as a purely functional lighting implement.

While the Bauhaus lamp emphatically proclaims its modernity, the **Painter-Stainers' Cup (75)** seems to echo the past. Yet the overt historical reference, to an English seventeenth-century steeple cup, has been restated in a way that would have made the object unmistakably contemporary when it was created in 1900-1. The cup was designed by Charles Robert Ashbee (1863-1942), whose influence on European twentieth-century metal-work was radical and far reaching. Ashbee was strongly attracted to the ideals and philosophies

Many of the most important and influential twentieth-century artists have produced books. *Klänge* (76) is by Wassily Kandinsky (1866-1944) and was published in 1913 in Munich, where the artist had lived since leaving his native Russia in 1897.

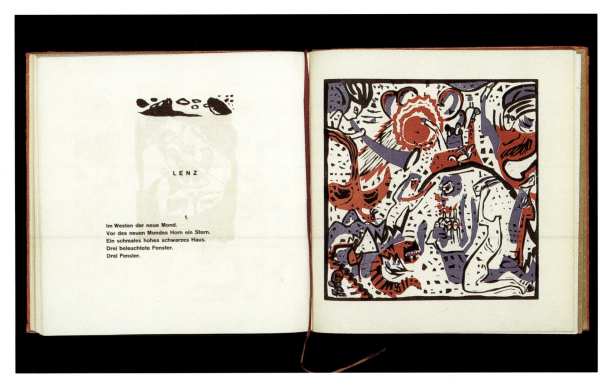

L E N Z

1.

Im Westen der neue Mond.
Vor des neuen Mondes Horn ein Stern.
Ein schmales hohes schwarzes Haus.
Drei beleuchtete Fenster.
Drei Fenster.

76. *Klänge* by Kandinsky
20th Century, Room 74
L.4200-1960
© ADAGP, Paris and DACS, London 1996.

of William Morris and the Arts and Craft movement. In 1888 he established the Guild of Handicraft, a co-operative venture that aimed to be socially democratic and to encourage the full creative potential of the craftsman. Despite these admirably egalitarian principles, Ashbee was the dominant designer of the Guild throughout the twenty years that it existed. His mature style, reflected in this silver cup set with semi-precious stones and enamelled decoration, displays a delicately subtle quality. The cup was commissioned in 1900 by Harris Heal, a member of the Heal family of furnishers, to commemorate his term of office as Master of the Painter-Stainers' Company.

Kandinsky was one of the first artists to paint in a purely abstract way, believing that colours and shapes had a spiritual dimension that transcended physical reality. *Klänge*, which means 'sounds', reflects Kandinsky's interest in the affinity between musical creation and painting. The illustrations in this limited edition book, said to be the first abstract compositions to be published, explore the relationship between sounds, colours and movement. While the book contains very innovative images and ideas, the methods used to produce it were extremely traditional. It was printed from woodblocks, the oldest printing technique.

77. Storage unit by Eames and Eames
20th Century, Room 73
◄ W.5-1991

Many of the items on display in the 20th Century Gallery are unique objects, or were made in only limited editions. Some, however, were designed to respond to the ever expanding needs of the mass market. This **storage unit (77)** was designed by American husband and wife team Charles (1907-78) and Ray (1913-88) Eames, who were particularly successful at creating modern furniture for mass-production. The complex technological processes they developed to make their furniture included the use of moulded plywood and cast metal. The plywood doors on this storage unit, of about 1949, have circular moulded depressions. As well as serving as a decorative motif, these give the doors added strength. The storage unit combines cupboards and open shelves, and can be used in the middle of a room as a space divider. The idea of modular, multi-purpose furniture was new in the 1950s and reflected changes in the way people lived. The Eames's own house in California even looked a little like this unit; it was constructed of solid, coloured wall panels interspersed with window walls, suspended in a metal frame.

ichard Slee (b.1946) is one of the most interesting British potters working today. Through work such as this 1983 piece *Cornucopia* (78), he has developed a very individual and witty ceramic style. The cornucopia is the horn of plenty, conventionally employed to represent many virtuous attributes. Here Slee has created a lighthearted, jaunty creature with maritime features. The freshness and brilliance of the coloured glazes, an important element in much of his work, are evidence of his technical mastery. Slee employs images and symbols derived from a wide range of ceramic traditions and art historical sources, as a vehicle for ironic commentary on the past, present and future role of ceramics in our culture.

78. *Cornucopia* **by Slee**
20th Century, Room 72
▲ C.253-1983

79. Bottle by Rie
20th Century, Room 71
Circ.1226-1967 ►

This **bottle (79)** is by another highly individual potter, Lucie Rie (1902-95). Rie arrived in London in 1938 as a Jewish refugee, leaving behind a sophisticated and intellectual Viennese background where she had already achieved considerable acclaim as a potter. For many years she shared her London studio with German refugee Hans Coper, who had been employed by Rie during the war to help make ceramic buttons and jewellery. Working and learning together they were to become the most dominant and pioneering forces in British studio pottery. The Museum has a collection of nearly 40 pieces of ceramics by Lucie Rie, including some important early work from Vienna, given to the Museum by the potter herself. Even in her eighties Rie continued to work extremely hard, experimenting relentlessly with rich and complex glazes which she applied to vases, bottles and bowls. This bottle, with its wide flaring rim, is instantly recognizable as a 'Lucie'. Her style is elegant, metropolitan, highly expressive and thoroughly modern.

The Ironwork Gallery

80. Ironwork Gallery
◄ Room 114

The Ironwork Gallery (80) houses the National Collection of decorative wrought and cast iron. The collection, which is one of the largest in the world, comes from all over Europe and ranges from the tenth century to the present day. It is enormously diverse and features large architectural pieces, firebacks and grates, candlesticks, chests, biscuit tins, locks and keys, and jewellery. Rarities include a Byzantine tenth-century folding seat, two seventeenth-century Venetian gondola prows and a unique eighteenth-century polished steel fireplace from Tula in Russia. Also on display are fragments from the gigantic Hereford cathedral screen. Designed by the architect Sir George Gilbert Scott (1811-78), the screen is one of the greatest Gothic Revival works in iron of the nineteenth century. It was acquired by the V&A in 1983, sadly in a very damaged state. The Museum plans to conserve this metal masterpiece and erect it as the focal point of the Gallery.

The Ironwork Gallery is the longest gallery in the Museum. With its series of arches, domes and vistas it is also one of the most architecturally striking. The newly displayed western wing of the Gallery, which contains the British, French and Italian ironwork, opened in 1994. To celebrate the occasion Albert Paley (b.1944), one of America's most important and innovative metalworkers, was commissioned to make a **forged iron bench (81)**. The bench was designed to incorporate different techniques of the forging process. The mahogany seat is supported by a sinuous and asymmetrical iron structure, this style being one for which Paley is famous. The bench is the first piece of Paley's work to be acquired by a British public collection.

81. Forged iron bench by Paley
Ironwork Gallery,
Room 114
▼ M.11-1995

The Ceramics Galleries

The Ceramics Galleries occupy the whole top floor of the Museum and some of the floor below. This enormous space is needed to display the Museum's remarkable collection of ceramics, which is by far the largest and most comprehensive in the world. This **bottle (82)** is one of the greatest treasures. It is one of the Museum's nine examples of 'Medici' porcelain, only sixty pieces of which have survived. It was made in an attempt to copy Chinese porcelain which first reached Europe, via Persia, in the sixteenth century. The blue-and-white porcelain was much coveted by the European wealthy élite, but the secret of its making was closely guarded by the Chinese and, before

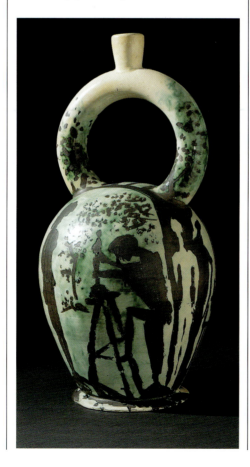

the development of chemical analysis, very secure. None the less, the possibility of discovery offered a challenge to which Francesco Maria de Medici, the second Grand Duke of Tuscany, applied his great wealth as well as his obsessive nature. From about 1575 Bernardo Buontalenti, the Grand Duke's universal craftsman at the workshops in the Boboli Gardens in Florence, was assisted in his experiments by members of the Fontana potting family from Urbino and by a 'Levantine' (probably a Turk). These imported craftsmen left their mark on the resulting 'porcelain', the forms of which often resemble Urbino *maiolica* (tin-glazed earthenware), and the decoration of which reflects the ceramic painting styles of China, Turkey and Italy. The material, though delicate and most beautiful, was not true porcelain, but consisted of a mixture of the materials available in Italy at the time: white china clay and ground Venetian glass. Although the experiment might be seen as a glorious failure, these first European porcelains are now considered the rarest, the most historically important and the most desirable of all.

This unusual **vase (83)** was made by one of the most famous artists of the twentieth century, Pablo Picasso (1881-1973). Although best-known for his painting and multimedia sculptures, Picasso's ceramics were an important part of his work, particularly in the 1950s. This vase was made in about 1954 at the Madoura Pottery on the French Riviera. Picasso first visited the Pottery in 1946 and continued to work there at various intervals for many years. The shape and decoration of the ceramics were designed by Picasso and then made for him by the Pottery. The curious shape of this vase, known as a Vase Aztèque, is based on a traditional native South American form. It is a unique work, decorated by Picasso, and is one of two by him in the Museum's Collections. The subject, *Artist at His Easel*, was a favourite of his and many versions of it are known from the mid- to later 1950s.

The Glass Gallery

The Glass Gallery (84) displays most of the Museum's 8,500 glass objects, and tells the story of glass from its beginnings in Ancient Egypt in around 2,500 BC right up to the present day. As the National Collection it includes not only comprehensive displays of art and commercial glass, but also a number of great masterpieces. Amongst the highlights are important groups of Renaissance Venetian enamelled glass, Dutch glass with masterly stipple-engraving, wheel-engraved German goblets, the earliest English lead-glass, English eighteenth- and nineteenth-century drinking and table glass, the most sumptuous High Victorian glass, Arts and Crafts glass and French Art Nouveau glass. The collection also includes wonderful examples of contemporary glass from Britain, Italy, Scandinavia and Czecho-slovakia. The whole dazzling display is complemented by a rippling glass balustrade by the American glass artist Danny Lane (b.1955).

One particularly precious object is the famous *Luck of Edenhall* (85). Glass drinking vessels hardly ever survive – or remain in one family – for long enough to acquire a legendary status so the successful passing of this vessel through many generations of the Musgrave family of Edenhall, Cumberland, is something of a miracle. Legend has it that this ancient beaker embodied the continuing prosperity of its owners. Telling the story in 1791, Sir William Musgrave wrote:

Tradition, our only guide here, says, that a

84. Glass Gallery
Room 131

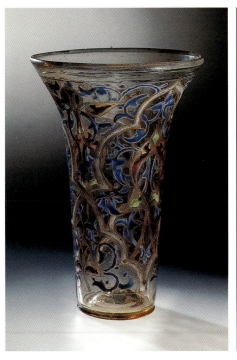

The dramatic blue glass sculpture *Arcus 1* (86) was designed and made by Stanislav Libenský (b.1921) and Jaraslova Brychtová (b.1924) in 1990-1. This Czechoslovakian husband and wife team are among the few really major figures in modern glassmaking. Their artistic achievement is of almost mythic proportion and their influence overshadows that of all other makers in their chosen field of monumental cast glass sculpture. In addition to this artistic and technical status, Libenský is the affectionately regarded and respected teacher of a whole generation of glass artists who are themselves world-leaders in this distinctively Czech form. As a team Libenský and Brychtová combine the skills of sculptor and glass technician, and have developed a technique which is particularly their own. *Arcus 1*, like all their works, is made in a mould taken from an original plaster sculpture. The mould is filled with chunks of raw glass, then heated until the glass melts, the finished form retaining the textural details of the original plaster as well as those of the effects of the intense heat.

85. *The Luck of Edenhall*
Glass, Room 131 C.1-1959

86. *Arcus 1* by Libenský and Brychtová
Glass, Room 131
C.4-1993 ▶

party of Fairies were drinking and making merry round a well near the Hall, called St. Cuthbert's well; but being interrupted by the intrusion of some curious people, they were frightened, and made a hasty retreat, and left the cup in question: one of the last screaming out,

     'If this cup should break or fall
     Farewell the Luck of Edenhall'.

The beaker is now known to be an exceptionally fine and pristine example of thirteenth-century Syrian luxury glassmaking. The beaker probably found its way to England in the baggage of a returning Crusader. While truth and romantic myth may have become interwoven over the centuries, it is clear that the survival of this rare and beautiful object is indeed lucky.

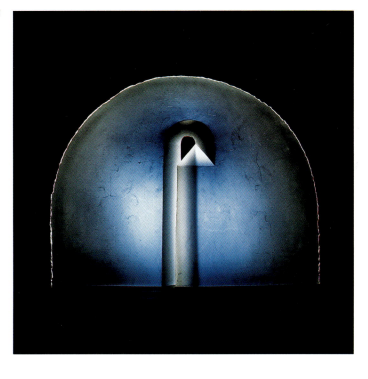

The Leighton Frescoes

The **Leighton Frescoes** were commissioned in 1868 as the central feature of the elaborate decorations of the Museum's South Court. The artist of the two enormous works, which each measure 10.7 metres (35 feet) across, was Frederic Leighton (1830-96), one of the most important figures in the late Victorian art world. Leighton's work is remarkable for its command of large-scale design, brilliant technique, intellectual sophistication, and skilful, often erotic depiction of the human body. The two frescoes, *The Arts of Industry as Applied to War* and *The Arts of Industry as Applied to Peace* (**87**), celebrate human artistic achievements. *War*, situated in Gallery 102, portrays the princes and courtiers of an Italian Renaissance city state setting out for battle. *Peace*, illustrated here, is set in a classical world of order and plenty. It is designed to evoke a sense of beauty rather than to illustrate a specific narrative, and depicts a central group of wealthy, elegant women dressing while, either side, workmen unload luxurious carpets and ceramics from barges.

The Jewellery Gallery

88. The Heneage Jewel
Jewellery Gallery,
Room 92
M.81-1935

**89. Necklace by
Ramshaw**
Jewellery Gallery,
Room 91
M.81-1982 ▶

The **Jewellery Gallery** contains one of the most resplendent and comprehensive collections of jewellery in the world. The **Heneage** or **Armada Jewel (88)** was given by Queen Elizabeth I to her Vice-Chamberlain Sir Thomas Heneage. Elizabeth and Heneage exchanged many gifts. She once said that whenever she wore an earring given to her by Sir Thomas she would not hear a word against him. The Heneage Jewel is a radiant declaration of the queen's majesty and achievement. The enamelled gold locket is set with diamonds and rubies and mounted with a profile of Queen Elizabeth in gold under rock crystal. On the reverse of the locket an enamelled boat represents the Ark of the English Church riding peacefully on the raging waves. Inside the locket is a portrait of the queen painted by Nicholas Hilliard (1547-1619), the leading miniaturist of the day. The jewel was traditionally believed to have been made in celebration of the defeat of the Spanish Armada in 1588. However, the costume depicted by Hilliard suggests that it was painted at a slightly later date, in about 1595.

The V&A has an extensive collection of contemporary jewellery including work by many of the leading artist-jewellers of Europe, America and the Far East. In the last three decades traditional forms and styles have been challenged, and the use of a diverse range of new materials, such as paper, acrylic and feathers, has been explored. This **necklace (89)** is by British jeweller Wendy Ramshaw (b.1939), who has been an influential figure since the 1960s. The linear and geometric nature of her work is influenced by industrial design and embodies the principles of Modernism, the movement that has influenced much twentieth-century practice. She often combines the use of both precious and non-precious materials, as in this necklace in which ceramic elements are arranged on rigid gold wires. It was made in 1981-2 during a collaborative project with Wedgwood.

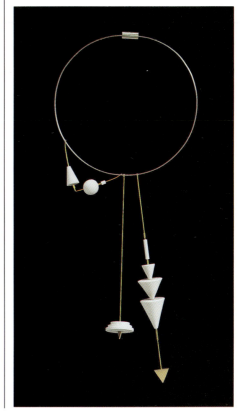

The Tapestry Gallery

90. Detail of the *Boar and Bear Hunt* tapestry
Tapestries, Room 94
T.204-1957

The Devonshire Hunting Tapestries (90) are a group of four magnificent Flemish tapestries dating from the mid-fifteenth century. These enormous works, each over 3 metres (10 feet) wide, depict men and women in fashionable dress of the early fifteenth century hunting in a forest. The tapestries formerly belonged to the Duke of Devonshire. The 6th Duke described using his 'spare tapestry' to insulate the Long Gallery at Hardwick Hall in the 1840s, a practice which saved these rare Gothic hangings from being discarded. This detail is from the *Boar and Bear Hunt Tapestry*, made in the 1420s, and shows men carrying special boar-spears, which have cross-bars designed to stop the charge of the boar and keep its deadly tusks at arm's length. Much of the charm of these scenes lies in the elaborate costume detail. The lady crossing the stream on the lower right has 'Monte le Desire' inscribed on her flowing sleeve. This is the opening line of a popular song of the period. The practice of embellishing one's clothes with such words was the medieval equivalent of having a stylish slogan printed on a T-shirt except that, in the tapestry, weaving on a horizontal loom has reversed the letters. The Devonshire Hunting Tapestries are a small part of the Museum's vast collection of European and Asian textiles, many of which are displayed in the **Textile Galleries**.

The Silver Gallery

The Silver Gallery displays the Museum's important collection of British and Continental silver which ranges from around 1300 to the present day. The **Mérode Cup (91)** was made in France or Burgundy in about 1400, and takes its name from the ancient Belgian family to whom it once belonged. The cup is made of silver gilt and is decorated with finely engraved birds, fruit and vine leaves. In the sides, cover and base are panels of the fragile and exquisite translucent enamel known as *plique à jour*. When the cup is placed on a shaft of light it appears to be set with miniature stained glass windows. Pieces decorated with this sort of enamel are known from inventories of people such as the great fourteenth century patron Jean, Duc de Berry, brother of Charles V of France. This cup, however, is the only one to survive from this period.

91. The Mérode cup
Silver Gallery, Room 65
403-1872

Prints, Drawings, Paintings and Photographs

Named after the first Director of the Museum, the Henry Cole Wing presently houses the V&A's collection of prints, drawings, paintings and photographs. The collection of British oil painting dates back to 1867 when John Sheepshank gave the Museum over 200 oil paintings and 300 watercolours by contemporary artists. This gift led to other donations. In 1888 a large collection of John Constable's (1776-1837) paintings, sketches and watercolours was presented to the Museum by the artist's eldest daughter. Constable was one of the foremost English landscape painters of the nineteenth century. *Flatford Mill* (**92**), painted in 1815, shows a barge under construction in a dry dock. The river Stour glimmers in the summer sunlight, while the labourers toil. The painting is essentially a tranquil pre-industrial landscape, but it is the numerous details which bring it to life: the little girl picking flowers to the right, the dog in the right foreground, the labourers' tools scattered across the ground and the cows in the far distance. Constable is recorded as saying that *Flatford Mill* was painted entirely in the open-air. If this is so, the painting is unique in being the only exhibition oil he painted wholly from life.

92. *Flatford Mill* **by Constable**
Constable, Henry Cole Wing Level 6
FA.27 ▲

93. *Design for a Park Gate* **by Chambers**
Print Room, Henry Cole Wing Level 5
3415 ▲ ▶

94. *Les Patineurs* **by Dufy**
Print Room, Henry Cole Wing Level 5
E.1028-1977 ▶
© DACS 1996.

Works on paper fade and deteriorate in the light, so they cannot be exhibited continuously. However, in addition to the ever-changing displays, there are nearly 1 million objects freely available through the **Print Room** on Level 5 of the Henry Cole Wing. They include designs, watercolours, drawings, photographs, prints, wallpapers, posters, greeting cards and fashion plates. Anyone can use the Print Room and no appointment is needed. The objects featured in this Guide are kept in a special box, so if you would like to look at them please ask at the Print Room desk.

The Print Room holds over 70,000 architectural drawings, including designs by Sir William Chambers (1723-96). *Design for a Park Gate* (**93**), executed in pen-and-ink and

watercolour, shows an elevation of a triumphal arch with a landscape in the background. Chambers was born in Göteborg, Sweden, the son of a Scottish merchant. He first trained as an architect in Paris in 1749 and then in Italy from 1750. After settling in England in 1755 he had immediate success and was appointed architectural tutor to the Prince of Wales in 1756. Chambers was particularly inspired by the architecture of classical Greece and Rome. His scholarly taste and attention to detail are exemplified in this design, which dates from about 1758.

Raoul Dufy's (1877-1953) design for a printed silk, *Les Patineurs* (**94**), is just one of many textile designs that can be viewed in the Print Room. The work of this French artist is characterized by the use of simple forms and bright colours. His decorative style was well-suited to the race-course and regatta scenes for which he is famous. In his early thirties Dufy met the French dress designer, Paul Poiret (1879-1944), who influenced his textile design. *Les Patineurs* (the skaters) was designed sometime between 1914 and 1920 for the Lyon silk manufacturer, Bianchini-Ferier, for whom Dufy worked from 1912. The design reveals the artist's characteristic taste for the world of sporting leisure as well as his use of distinctive outlines and areas of pure colour.

95. *Feeling more snowy behind the ears than ever he had before* **by Shepard**
Print Room, Henry Cole
Wing Level 5
E.649-1973

96. *Jarrow Youth* **by Killip**
Print Room, Henry Cole
Wing Level 5
852-1978

Winnie-the-Pooh is probably one of the most popular characters ever created in the history of children's literature. Over 270 of the illustrations Ernest Howard Shepard (1879-1976) made for A. A. Milne's books are available in the Print Room. *Feeling more snowy behind the ears than ever he had before* (**95**) comes from chapter 1 of *The House at Pooh Corner*, published in 1928.

The V&A was the first Museum in Britain to collect photography as an art form, and its collections now number over 300,000 objects. *Jarrow Youth* (**96**) is one of the best-known images by British photographer Chris Killip (b.1946). Taken in north-east England, where Killip lived and worked in the 1970s and 1980s, this image captures a moment in British culture. The photograph was taken in 1976 at a time when abandoned 'skinhead' youth seemed ready for every excess, including the political. Killip habitually works with a large camera in order to represent his subjects with magnifying-glass clarity. Here he presents an image that symbolizes both vulnerability and potential. This, and other equally powerful photographs by Killip, can be seen in the Print Room.

The V&A collection of oil paintings, water-colours and drawings was greatly enriched by the 1900 bequest from Constantine Alexander Ionides (1833-1900), a Greek cloth merchant and stockbroker. A large group of paintings from this collection are displayed on Level 4 of the Henry Cole Wing. Many of them are French, but Ionides was also a patron of a number of British artists including Edward Coley Burne-Jones (1833-98). In 1870 Ionides commissioned Burne-Jones to paint *The Mill* (**97**). The painting depicts three maidens dancing to music by a river. In the background there are mill buildings and some nude male figures bathing. The model for one of the three graces, Aglaia Coronio, was Ionides' sister. Of the other two models, Maria Zambaco was Burne-Jones' lover, while Marie Spartali was an artist. The highly decorative style of *The Mill* and the mood it evokes of dreamy romance is characteristic of many of Burne-Jones's pictures.

The V&A probably has the greatest collection of British miniatures in the world. The portrait of **Jane Small (98)** is by Hans Holbein (1497-1543), who was the first artist to perfect painting in this way. Holbein was already an artist of international stature when in 1532, forced by religious unrest abroad and a consequent lack of patrons, he came to England from Switzerland. Here he found success and recognition, becoming court painter to Henry VIII in 1535. He held this position until his death. It was during his time in England that Holbein was taught to paint 'in miniature', the term used at that time to describe not the size of the painting, but the nature of the pigments used. This exquisite technique of painting in watercolour on vellum, the fine parchment produced from the skin of a calf, originated in illuminated manuscripts. Jane Small was the wife of a prosperous cloth worker in the City of London. For Holbein to paint a woman outside the élite confines of the royal court was very unusual. She is depicted as a simply dressed young woman who, according to the Latin inscription, is aged 23. She holds a leaf and at her neck is a red carnation which is possibly a reference to a betrothal. Despite her modest rank Jane Small is still a commanding figure, and serves as a striking example of Holbein's ability to characterize his sitters.

97. *The Mill* by Burne-Jones
Paintings, Henry Cole Wing
Level 4
CAI.8

98. *Jane Small* by Holbein
Portrait Miniatures,
Henry Cole Wing
Level 4
P.40-1934

The Dutch artist Rembrandt van Rijn (1606-69) occupies as unique a position in the history of prints as he does in the history of painting. Etchings such as *The Virgin and Child with a Cat* (**99**), of 1654, represent the very pinnacle of printmaking as a creative art form and provide a standard against which all others have to be compared. It is to Rembrandt that generations of etchers have constantly looked for inspiration. The V&A is very fortunate to have in its collection not only one of the earliest impressions of this etching, but the actual copper plate from which the image was taken. This rare combination enriches both our understanding of the process involved in etching and the working methods of one of its greatest exponents. The print and plate are one of the highlights of the Printmaking Gallery.

Although most of the displays in the Henry Cole Wing are devoted to paintings, drawing and prints, the building also houses a gallery dedicated to the work of the great American architect Frank Lloyd Wright (1885-1955). Wright's career spanned sixty years, but he built nothing in Europe, making the **Office for Edgar J. Kaufmann (100)** the only example of his architecture this side of the Atlantic. The office was designed for the proprietor of a Pittsburgh department store in 1935-7, and was given to the Museum by his son. Wright designed every detail of the room so that the